To:

_____

From:

_____

Date:

_____

The golden rule is of no use whatsoever unless you realize that it is your move.

ANONYMOUS

—⚬⚬⚬—

All of the world is full of suffering, it is full also of the overcoming of it.

HELEN KELLER

Actions speak louder than words.

POOR RICHARD'S ALMANAC, 1766

—✦—

*The length and breadth of our influence upon others
depends upon the depth of our concern for others.*

ANONYMOUS

Life's Interruptions
God's Opportunities

LESSONS FROM THE GOOD SAMARITAN

LARRY JONES

WITH KEN ABRAHAM

J. COUNTRYMAN®
NASHVILLE, TENNESSEE
WWW.JCOUNTRYMAN.COM

TABLE OF CONTENTS

Let God Interrupt
Your Life

—◦◦◦—

A number of years ago, Charles Schultz drew a powerful cartoon in his *Peanuts* comic strip. In it, Snoopy is seen standing in a snowstorm, shivering beside an empty food dish. As he looks longingly toward the house, Lucy comes outside and says to him, "Go in peace, be warmed and filled!" Then she turns around and goes back into the house, leaving a confused Snoopy still cold, still shivering, and still hungry.

Apparently, Lucy doesn't recognize the opportunity before her. After all, it isn't her job to care for the dog. Snoopy belongs to Charlie Brown; let him worry. Lucy has a schedule to meet, an agenda to fill. She has no time for interruptions! She doesn't have the energy or the resources to invest herself in someone else's problem.

In one of the most familiar stories in the Bible, Jesus tells about three busy men whose lives are interrupted by another person's problem. Two of those men—a priest and a Levite, both very religious, indeed—decide not to allow life's interruptions to detour them from their own hectic agendas. They have no allowance for delays, no room for interruptions. No doubt the same full schedule holds true for the despised Samaritan, a man whose family isn't even from that part of the country. But the

Samaritan recognizes the wounded traveler as an opportunity to do the work of God, and Jesus uses that man to make His point: "Your neighbor is anyone in need." That man—an unnamed fellow who allowed God to turn an interruption into an opportunity—has been known ever since as "The Good Samaritan."

MORE THAN EIGHT HUNDRED MILLION PEOPLE—
ABOUT ONE-FIFTH OF THE POPULATION OF THE WORLD'S
DEVELOPING NATIONS—ARE MALNOURISHED,
AND TWO HUNDRED MILLION OF THEM ARE CHILDREN.
(UNITED NATIONS DEVELOPMENT PROGRAM)

Interruptions are God's Opportunities

J esus constantly was interrupted in His ministry. Crowds, disciples, the poor, the sick, the dying—all clamored for His attention. Amazingly, Jesus didn't mind! He welcomed hurting people and the interruptions their needs represented. His style of ministry actually invited intrusion. Jesus saw people as an opportunity to do His work, rather than as a hindrance to His work.

In fact, many of Jesus' miracles were performed when He was interrupted. Think about it. His first miracle was the turning of water into wine at a wedding in Cana. Jesus was interrupted while celebrating with the other guests at the reception.

His second miracle was the healing of an official's son. Remember when it happened? Jesus was interrupted while journeying across Galilee.

The lame man walking. The paralyzed man rising. The dead child that Jesus brought back to life. Interruptions, every one. Jesus took a few moments to heal human conditions that had been endured for years—skin decayed by leprosy, ears clogged with deafness, eyes caked from disease, open sores, bleeding cuts, deformed and shriveled limbs. Lazarus freed. People fed. A legion of demons defeated. All of these astonishing miracles were accomplished when Jesus was interrupted.

Behind every one of life's interruptions is an opportunity to do the work of God.

Why didn't Jesus mind being interrupted? Because Jesus loved people. He was approachable, easy to talk to, easy to like—how unlike many of us who claim to represent God today. Moreover, Jesus responded to every interruption by listening, caring, reaching out, and touching. He knew what we often forget: Behind every one of life's interruptions is an opportunity to do the work of God.

It Doesn't Take Much

M ore than twenty years ago, God used a youngster in Haiti to interrupt my life and bring about the ministry of Feed The Children. I shudder to think what blessings I would have missed had I not stopped to see the eyes of Jesus and hear the voice of Christ in that little boy.

In January, 1979, I was speaking at a church in Port Au Prince, Haiti, the poverty capital of the world. It was hot and sticky—about 95 degrees and 95 percent humidity. One night, a little boy named Jerry, whom I had met earlier in the week, emerged from the shadows of the street as I approached my hotel. Jerry stuck out his skinny arm in my direction. "Lorry," he said, mispronouncing my name, "can you spare a nickel?"

"Sure, Jerry. What for?"

"So I can go to that store over there and buy me a roll," Jerry replied. "I haven't eaten all day."

His words rattled around in my head like rocks in a hub cap. I had just preached a sermon on the love and generosity of God. How could I not acknowledge this child's need?

I willingly pressed money into Jerry's hand and off he went, running full speed toward the store. But the little guy must have been a budding marketer, because he stopped abruptly in his tracks, turned around, and came back to tug at my heartstrings.

"Lorry," he asked again. "Do you also got three cents?"

When I inquired what he needed that for, he smiled and replied, "Well, for three cents, that store will break open the roll and put butter on both sides of the bread!"

Of course, I gave Jerry the coins, and he started off again. But this time I stopped the youngster. "How much for a Coke?" I inquired. "You gotta wash it down."

"A drink costs twelve cents," Jerry's eyes brightened with hope as he spoke. I laid that amount in the small, outstretched hand. A mere twenty cents bought little Jerry's meal that day—not a nutritious meal, but a meal nevertheless. I later learned that the bread, butter, and drink comprised Jerry's only meal that day!

As I went back to my hotel to prepare another sermon, only one passage of Scripture came to mind: "I was hungry and you gave Me food" (Matthew 25:35).

Upon my return to Oklahoma, I compared the abundance in America's overflowing grain elevators to the meagerness in Haiti, just a few hours away by plane. I became angry when I thought about how our government subsidized farmers not to grow food, while this neighboring country so desperately needed it to survive.

I did some research and discovered that at that time, America had thirty-five million metric tons of wheat in grain elevators. Can you imagine how much it costs American taxpayers to store that stuff? Why not use some of this grain to help feed hungry children? So I took action!

Everywhere I could get an audience, I asked, "Can you spare some change for a friend of mine in Haiti?" I appeared on a Christian television program and talked about the gross inequity of our having such enormous surplus when children just a few hours away had nothing eat.

The response was overwhelming. I hadn't specifically asked people to provide wheat for the impoverished people in Haiti, but some farmers donated more than fifty truckloads of wheat in a matter of weeks—that's over two million pounds! Of course, that created another interesting situation: I had only a two–car garage.

Where was I going to store all that wheat until I could make arrangements to transport it?

Transport it? Oh my! I had never even sent something as small as a shoebox overseas, and now I had two million pounds of wheat to transport. The problems staggered my mind, but from the beginning, I was convinced that this was God's work, not mine. And God did not disappoint; He raised up a man who owned a tractor–trailer truck to move the wheat to the shipyards. From there we arranged to have the wheat sent to the pastor in Haiti. A man in the United States donated some commercial grinding apparatus to grind the wheat into flour for bread, and he even volunteered to go to Haiti to help set up the equipment. It was a shaky beginning, but God helped us to deliver the wheat to people who needed it desperately.

My wife, Frances, and I hadn't planned to make Feed The Children our life's work. We just felt compelled to feed hungry children, so we started doing it. We worked for two years before we even gave our organization a name. I had no idea that a nine-year-old boy asking for a single roll of bread would grow into Feed The Children's annual distribution of nearly 140 million pounds of food, medicines, and other items for needy children in the United States and around the world [i].

And to think it all began with an interruption.

The wounded won't wait.

Whether your neighbor needs a mere nickel for food, or if someone requests clothing, shelter, or other help; whether it comes from a tug on your heart at work, or a phone call in the middle of the night, an interruption by someone in need will probably inconvenience you. You might fail to realize its necessity. And because the interruption most likely will require time, energy, or resources, you may fail to realize its urgency.

But the wounded won't wait. They demand our full attention. We need to care about others as surely as we need to breathe. We need to recognize the opportunity and accept the responsibility to do the work of God in our world. We need to learn the life lessons from the Good Samaritan that Jesus wants us to know. Most of all, we need to be like Jesus.

I was hungry, and you formed a humanities club and discussed my hunger.
I was imprisoned, and you crept off quietly to your chapel and prayed for my release.
I was naked, and in your mind you debated the morality of my appearance.
I was sick, and you knelt and thanked God for your health.
I was homeless, and you preached to me the spiritual shelter of the love of God.
I was lonely and you left me alone to pray for me.
You seem so holy, so close to God, but I'm still very hungry, and lonely, and cold.

ANONYMOUS

The chief enemy to compassion is "busyness."
ANONYMOUS

Divine Interruptions

———— ❧ ————

"A certain man went down from Jerusalem to Jericho, and fell among thieves,
who stripped him of his clothing, wounded him, and departed, leaving him half dead.
Now by chance a certain priest came down that road. And when he saw him, he passed by on the other
side. Likewise a Levite, when he arrived at the place, came and looked, and passed by on the other side.
But a certain Samaritan, as he journeyed, came where he was.
And when he saw him, he had compassion."

LUKE 10:30-33

The Timing of a Miracle

I had never really thought about a certain question before Ken
Wilson, the former editor of the *Christian Herald* magazine,
broached the subject to me. A quiet, unassuming man, Ken was
accompanying our crew as we filmed a television program in the Rift
Valley outside of Nairobi, Kenya. We were standing under a tree,
trying to stay in the shade as much as possible, when Ken asked:
"do you know when the miracles of Jesus took place?"

"Well, I've read about His miracles, but I'm not sure I know
what you're going to tell me," I replied.

"The miracles of Jesus took place when He was interrupted,"
Ken said quietly.

His words were soft, but they set off an explosion in my heart.
As often as I had read the New Testament, it had never occurred to
me that almost every time Jesus performed a miracle, it was an
"interruption" in His schedule. I thought about the signs we often

display on our hotel door: Do Not Disturb. More importantly, I became convicted about the Do Not Disturb sign I had placed on the door of my heart all too many times.

The great preacher and Bible expositor Allan Redpath put it this way: "Thy kingdom come? My kingdom must go!" In other words, if I really want to see God use my life for His glory and to the benefit of other people, my agenda must take a lower position on my priority list. This message also applies to our churches.

Theologian Karl Barth pointedly said, "The last hiding place from God on earth is in the church." We can get so busy for God that we miss what matters most to the heart of God.

Instead of studying the steps of Jesus,
I like to see what I can learn about the stops of Jesus.
GEORGE GARDNER

ONLY NINE PERCENT OF THE WORLD'S POPULATION SPEAKS ENGLISH,
YET NINETY-FOUR PERCENT OF OUR ORDAINED MINISTERS
WORK WITH THAT NINE PERCENT.

Can We Really Make a Difference?

B eing able to do so little in the face of such staggering need invariably leaves me frustrated. Interviewers add to my feelings of helplessness with the constant query: "do you think you are making a dent in the hunger problem?"

I don't work on problems; I help people. Jesus is my model. He did not heal every sick person in Palestine, nor did He feed all the hungry. He did not set right every injustice, nor did He spend His every waking moment attempting to do those things. He slept and went on retreats. He attended parties and led seminars. He lived life in its ordinary dimensions, and I believe He expects me to do the same.

But—and here is the test of my faithfulness—He never turned away from helping anyone who came within the scope of His awareness. I can do that.[ii]

The British missionary pioneer C. T. Studd was born into luxury, comfort, and ease; he was educated at the best schools and became a professional athlete. But God interrupted his life, and Studd renounced fame, wealth, and position to follow Christ's leading. By the time he died on the mission field, he had spent forty-six years serving God in China, India, and Africa. The motivation of his life is found in these four lines:

Some wish to live within the sound
Of church or chapel bell,
I want to run a rescue shop
Within a yard of hell.

                                                        C. T. Studd

A 'New' Law?

One of the most popular television shows of the 1990s was *Seinfeld*, a situation comedy ostensibly "about nothing." The final episode of the *Seinfeld* show aired at the end of the 1998 TV season, and while it, too, was supposedly about nothing, it served up a poignant reminder to its viewers. In the final show, each of the main characters received a one-year sentence for failing to help someone who was being robbed. The chronically callous group had violated the town's new "Good Samaritan" law, which required people to assist anyone in danger as long at was reasonable to do so.

However, the law to assist someone in need is as old as the tablets Moses brought down from Mount Sinai. There's nothing new about it. But just in case you can't recall the story and why Jesus told it, let me refresh your memory.

> And behold, a certain lawyer stood up and tested Him, saying, "Teacher, what shall I do to inherit eternal life?" He said to him, "What is written in the law? What is your reading of it?" So he answered and said, " 'You shall love the Lord your God with all your heart, with all your soul, with all your strength, and with all your mind,' and 'your neighbor as yourself.' " And He said to him, "You have answered rightly; do this and you will live." But he, wanting to justify himself, said to Jesus, "And who is my neighbor?" Then Jesus answered and said: "A certain man went down from Jerusalem to Jericho, and fell among thieves, who stripped him of his clothing, wounded him, and departed, leaving him half dead. "Now by chance a certain priest came down that road. And when he saw him, he passed by on the other side. "Likewise a Levite, when he arrived at the place, came and looked, and passed by on the other side. "But a certain Samaritan, as he journeyed, came where he was. And when he saw him, he had compassion. "So he went to him and bandaged his wounds, pouring on oil and wine; and he set him

on his own animal, brought him to an inn, and took care of him. "On the next day, when he departed, he took out two denarii, gave them to the innkeeper, and said to him, 'Take care of him; and whatever more you spend, when I come again, I will repay you.' "So which of these three do you think was neighbor to him who fell among the thieves?" And he said, "He who showed mercy on him." Then Jesus said to him, "Go and do likewise".

LUKE 10:25–37

The lawyer who sparked this story seemed sincere when he asked Jesus what he must do to inherit eternal life. As a devout student of the Old Testament, the lawyer probably wore a phylactery, a small leather box containing verses of Scripture and strapped to either the forehead or the left hand. The specific passages contained in the little box were Exodus 13:1-10 and Exodus 13:11-16; and Deuteronomy 6:4-9 and Deuteronomy 11:13-21.

When the lawyer answered Jesus' question about the Law, he quoted from the passages in Deuteronomy, and he even threw in a portion from Leviticus 19:18: "You shall love your neighbor as yourself." Jesus acknowledged the lawyer's knowledge of the Scripture and then quoted another passage, "Do this and live" (Genesis 42:18). In a sense Jesus was saying, "You're wearing the Scriptures on your body, now do what they say."

But then, the lawyer did as most of us do. He tried to "justify" himself, looking for loopholes, by asking the loaded question, "Well, who is my neighbor?" Many of us try to do the same thing.

"Sure, I'd love to impact the world, but . . ."

"I'd like to help make a difference in somebody's life, but . . ."

"Who am I to try to attempt such a big project?"

"I don't even know where to start."

"What can one person do, anyhow?"

"I'm already giving as much as I can."

We can all justify our deeds and our actions—or our inaction. You don't need to be an attorney to do that. Love will find a way; indifference will find an excuse.

Love will find a way; indifference will find an excuse.

A reporter for a major television station was interviewing people on the street one day. He approached a well-dressed, successful-looking man and asked, "What are the two most pressing problems in America?"

The man answered, "I don't know and I don't care."

"You are absolutely right!" the reporter replied.

That's the attitude of indifference. An "I don't know and I don't care" mentality pervades our culture. No one, anywhere, is immune from the comfort zone of unconcern. People know that it's easier to sit down and take notice, than it is to stand up and take action. People look, but don't see; hear, but don't listen; talk a good line, but don't walk it.

We are quick to toss out glib quotes like, "Give a man a fish, and you feed him for a day. Teach him to fish, and you feed him for a lifetime." Many of these pious sounding platitudes, however, are little more than smoke screens to mask our unconcern. We've never tried to teach a man to fish who is being shot at while he's trying to bait the hook. We've also forgotten that oftentimes the would-be

In America, you are not required to offer food to the hungry, or shelter to the homeless. There is no ordinance forcing you to visit the lonely, or comfort the infirm. Nowhere in the Constitution does it say you have to provide clothing for the poor. In fact, one of the nicest things about living here in America is that you really don't have to do anything for anybody.

AUTHOR UNKNOWN

fisherman doesn't own a fishing pole, or a line, a hook, or any bait. And by the way, he doesn't have a pond either.

In the United States, we don't have to do anything about hurting people. Instead, we can assess blame, pass the buck, or find an excuse for not doing what we know in our hearts is right.

But Jesus wasn't buying any excuses when He answered the lawyer's question. Instead, He told a simple, yet profound story with many life lessons as we think about how good God has been to us, and what we can do to help others.

Jesus told of a man who set out on a business trip down one of the most notorious routes in Israel, the twenty–mile stretch from Jerusalem to Jericho. It was a treacherous passage, with rocky crags, twists and turns, and encounters with thieves along the desolate path. The road's reputation was so bad it was known as "The Bloody Way," and few travelers dared to go it alone.

Not surprisingly, the man in Jesus' story was accosted, stripped of his clothing, robbed, and severely beaten along the Jerusalem–Jericho road. No doubt, as Jesus spoke, the attorney was already assessing the situation, condescendingly musing, "He should have known better than to take a trip like that alone. He has no one to blame but himself!"

Maybe so, but Jesus wasn't going to let the lawyer off the hook so easily.

Jesus told of three men who discovered the beaten traveler—a priest, a Levite, and a Samaritan. All three men saw the helpless traveler lying along the roadside.

The priest took one look and passed by on the other side of the road, trying to get as far from the man—and possibly more danger—as he could. Perhaps the priest thought the man was dead and that if he touched him, he would be ceremonially unclean for seven days and could not serve in the temple. Or maybe he felt he was too good to get involved in such an obviously messy situation. For whatever reason, the priest put himself above the desperation and pain of a man. And he passed on by—on the other side.

The Levite came along. This man was a member of the family of Levi, the group of Hebrews that God initially set apart to serve Him and the people. Maybe the Levite thought the man crumpled in a pile was merely a ploy, part of a plot to rip him off. It was not above the morality of some in those days to pretend that they were hurting, so they could lure good-hearted people into compromising situations. "No, this might be dangerous," the Levite might have thought. "I can't risk it. I see the need, but I might get hurt. I might get ripped off. If I stop, I might not be able to fulfill my obligations." In other words, he was not willing to be interrupted. And the Levite, too, passed by—on the other side.

Then came the Samaritan. Although descendants of Abraham like the Jews, the Samaritans were considered the scum of the earth, as far as pious Jews were concerned. Generations before, they had broken fellowship with God's family and ever since had worshiped their own gods around the small city of Samaria, in the north near the Sea of Galilee. The Samaritans were despised as backslidden half-breeds by orthodox Jews, and the two groups typically avoided each other. The attorney to whom Jesus was speaking probably anticipated the pagan rogue approaching the body would kick the guy when he was down.

The Samaritan himself was alone and a long way from home. Why should he interrupt his journey with somebody who was

Men are all alike in their promises. It is only in their deeds that they differ.
MOLIERE

hurting, somebody he didn't know, and likely would never know?

Imagine how the lawyer must have gulped hard as Jesus described the compassionate actions of the Samaritan. Notice, the action words: the Samaritan saw the man and felt compassion. He came to him, bandaged his wounds, poured oil and wine on them. He then lifted him onto his own animal, took him to an inn, took care of him, and paid the innkeeper to allow the bruised man to stay there until he recuperated. He even promised to pay for any further expenses the innkeeper might incur in helping to get the beaten man back on his feet.

The Samaritan didn't just talk about loving his fellow man. He didn't purchase another "What Would Jesus Do?" T-shirt, hat, wristband, or bumper sticker. Instead, the Samaritan put his beliefs into action. He did something about the situation even though it cost him time, effort, possibly his reputation, and certainly his money. We don't know for sure, but it's entirely possible that he missed his appointment because he helped somebody.

Surely, the priest and the Levite were good men. They probably were grieved at the sight of another victim along the way. As the great expositor William Barclay points out, "No doubt the priest and the Levite felt a pang of pity for the wounded man, but they did nothing. Compassion, to be real compassion, must issue in deeds."[iii]

After telling the story of the Good Samaritan, Jesus turned the question back to the lawyer, asking, "Which of these three proved to be a neighbor to the man who fell into the robbers' hands?"

How the lawyer must have cringed as he replied, "The one who showed mercy to him."

But Jesus wasn't going to allow the man to be content with merely coming to the correct conclusions, mouthing the right answers. Jesus expects right actions. "Go and do the same," He told the lawyer. That has been our mandate ever since, and remains so to this day. If we miss that greatest of all life-lessons from this story, we will have missed the whole point.

Charity begins at home, but should not end there.
THOMAS FULLER, M.D.

NEARLY THIRTY-FIVE THOUSAND CHILDREN
UNDER FIVE YEARS OF AGE DIE EACH DAY IN DEVELOPING COUNTRIES,
MAINLY FROM MALNUTRITION AND OTHER PREVENTABLE CAUSES.
(UNICEF)

The Green Light of Faith

My commitment to Christ has been a green light of faith—not a yellow caution light or a red stoplight. This green light says, "Go into all the world and share what you have found in Me."

God has used interruptions several times to get my attention and direct me along the right road, but each time I learned a little more about Him and about my destiny in His service.

For instance, when I was a boy, every year I attended vacation Bible school. The summer I was five, our arts and crafts project was to create a "stained glass" bird. I was delighted with my project and couldn't wait for Mom and Dad to see it, too, but I stumbled while carrying it. My beautiful bird slipped and shattered into a million pieces. I was embarrassed, hurt, and angry. Huge tears dripped down my face. My teacher instantly came over to comfort me, and at that moment, my small mind grasped a big truth: tears can be erased with love.

Tears need to be dried with love.

All week long, our teachers had been telling us about Jesus and our need for accepting God's gift of love. I had listened attentively along with the other kids, and then, suddenly, I could see that message reflected in the eyes of this wonderful teacher. Love meant it was okay to stumble, because you could pick yourself up and start over—and God would help you! So that was the gospel!

Sitting on a teacher's lap in vacation Bible school, I grasped the truth of John 3:16: "For God so loved the world that He gave His only begotten Son, that whoever believes in Him should not perish but have everlasting life." I asked Jesus to come into my life; as much as I knew how I put my trust in Him, and committed to Him.

At that moment, I discovered the answer to the lawyer's question: "What must I do to inherit eternal life?" Somehow I knew that if I should die, I'd go to heaven, but until then I wanted to do the things that pleased God. That encounter with God has colored every aspect of my life from that day on.

Later, when I was thirteen years old and attending a summer church camp, I decided during a special consecration service to commit my life and future plans to God. But the next morning I was terrified. I couldn't believe what I had done! I went to find my preacher. "Pastor, do you remember that paper I signed last night?"

"Yes, I sure do, Larry," he said, beaming. "I've got it right here."

"Well, tear it up!"

"You're not serious?"

"Yes, sir. Tear it up."

And he did.

I was honest in what I wanted to do. I really wanted to go into the ministry . . . someday. I just wasn't ready to do it then! Sure, I knew and followed all the "thou shalts and thou shalt nots," but it would take a few more years of growing before I discovered how to trust God completely and allow Him to be first in my life.

That full commitment happened during my senior year in high school. Growing up in the Midwest, my upbringing was typical of boys in our area—go to church three times a week and play basketball every moment in between.

Everything changed during my last semester of high school. A week before I was to take the physical for an Air Force Academy appointment, I fell during a basketball scrimmage and snapped the bones in my forearm. It was the biggest disappointment of my young life. I didn't just like basketball; I loved basketball. More than a broken arm, I had a broken heart.

But my disappointment became God's appointment. I don't believe God caused me to break my arm, but I do believe He used the incident to get my attention. As I sat on the sidelines waiting for the bones to heal, I had time to think about my priorities. I had thought my biggest decision that year would be where I would attend college, but God lifted my eyes to a higher level. I had wanted to find an education; God wanted me to find a life.

My disappointment became God's appointment.

Within weeks, I reaffirmed my intention to enter the ministry. It was not a complicated decision, but more of, "Well, Lord, I've had this life for seventeen years, and I've basically done what I wanted. Now I give my life to you."

It's amazing what God can do when His children trust and believe in Him!

What is the secret to eternal life? To love God with all our hearts, and to love our neighbors as ourselves.

We've been missing this point in our churches. Some people go to church for years, and remain unsatisfied. "I don't get it," they say. "There has to be more to living than just waiting to die."

And they're right. Church provides our vertical relationship with God. Loving our neighbor is the horizontal expression of our love for God. If you draw the vertical and the horizontal lines together you get an

which stands for the "Love of God expressed through us." We will never truly know the love of God in our lives the way He wants us to know it, until we see Christ in our neighbors.

The 'Other' John 3:16

The lawyer who confronted Jesus was not just asking how he could live forever. Heaven would be an awful place if all we had was an eternal quantity of time, with no improvement in the quality of our lives. Ordinarily, when somebody asks how he or she might have eternal life, we tell them, "Believe on the Lord Jesus Christ, and you will be saved."

But this lawyer was probing much deeper. Being steeped in the Scriptures, he probably knew the answer to his initial question. He was really asking, "How can I have the highest quality of life possible here on earth and in heaven to come?"

The key to having that sort of abundant life is found in "the other John 3:16." The Apostle John wrote five books in the New Testament—the Gospel of John, the book of Revelation, and three short, insightful little letters. In 1 John 3:16 we read, "By this we know love, because He laid down His life for us. And we also ought to lay down our lives for the brethren."

Most Christians can readily quote the former verse, but in all my years of speaking and traveling all around the world, I've met only five people who could quote the latter.

We don't memorize that verse, but we should. John says, that because Jesus died for us, we ought to be willing to give up our lives for others. If we want to have real life, abundant life, we must lay down our lives for our brothers and sisters who are hurting in this world. How are we to do that? John explains further: "But whoever has this world's goods, and sees his brother in need, and shuts up his heart from him, how does the love of God abide in him? My little children, let us not love in word or in tongue, but in deed and in truth" (1 John 3:17–18).

This was the second great lesson Jesus wanted to get across to the lawyer who asked how he could have life to the max—if you want to have abundant life, you must be willing to give yourself away.

> By this we know love, because He laid down His life for us. And we also ought to lay down our lives for the brethren. But whoever has this world's goods, and sees his brother in need, and shuts up his heart from him, how does the love of God abide in him? My little children, let us not love in word or in tongue, but in deed and in truth.
>
> 1 JOHN 3:16-18

ACCORDING TO THE PEARSON COMMISSION,
THIRTY-FOUR PERCENT OF THE WORLD'S POPULATION HAS
EIGHTY-FOUR PERCENT OF THE GROSS NATIONAL PRODUCT.
SIXTY-SIX PERCENT OF THE WORLD'S POPULATION HAS ONLY
SIXTEEN PERCENT OF THE GROSS NATIONAL PRODUCT.

Recognizing Our Responsibility

—∽∾∼—

"The man wanted to show that the way he was living was right.
So he said to Jesus, 'And who is my neighbor?'"

LUKE 10:29, NCV

Love Must Take Risks

The story is told of a man who worked late every night, and to get home more quickly, he often took a shortcut through a city park. One evening he heard some rustling and muffled cries in the nearby bushes, sounding like a girl was being raped. He started to help the young woman, but then he stopped short, realizing that the attacker might have a gun or a knife. So he waited. Finally he heard the heavy footsteps of someone running away.

He hurried into the bushes, calling out, "Honey, are you okay?"

The voice came back, "Daddy, is that you?"

Had he known it was his daughter in trouble, regardless if the rapist had a weapon, the father would have plunged into the bushes to rescue his child. Similarly, if we are really to love our neighbor as we love ourselves, our love must take risks.

The love of our neighbor is the only door out of the dungeon of self.
GEORGE MCDONALD

Don't you wonder what might have happened if the priest in the Good Samaritan story had recognized the person in the ditch? We sometimes have such a narrow focus, as if we are wearing blinders. We tend to take care of "our own" or our own "kind." But the Good Samaritan risked crossing ethnic, religious, and political boundaries to help someone in need. And Jesus says, "Go and do likewise" (Luke 10:37).

Love must take risks or it's not love.

LARRY JONES

We have made the slogan "Charity begins at home" a part of our religion—although it was invented by a Roman pagan, and is directly contrary to the story of the Good Samaritan. Charity begins where the need is greatest and the crisis is most dangerous.

Frank C. Laubach

All men are our neighbors, and we are to love them as ourselves. We are to do this on the basis of creation, even if they are not redeemed, for all men have value because they are made in the image of God. Therefore they are to be loved even at great cost.

Francis Schaeffer

All Are Ours

I heard a story on the radio about an event in Bosnia that has implications for all of us. A reporter was covering the tragic conflict in Sarajevo when he saw a little girl shot by a sniper. The reporter threw down his pad and pencil, rushed to the man who was holding the child, and helped them both into his car.

As the reporter stepped on the accelerator, racing to the hospital, the man cradling the bleeding child said, "Hurry, my friend! My child is still alive!" A moment or two later, he implored, "Hurry, my friend! My child is still breathing." A moment later, "Hurry, my friend! My child is still warm." As the car careened into the hospital lane, the man cried, "Hurry, oh, God, my child is getting cold!"

Just as they got the little girl to the hospital, she died. The man turned to the reporter and said, "This is a terrible task for me. I must go tell a father that his child is dead. He will be heartbroken."

The reporter was amazed. He looked at the grieving man, and said, "I thought she was your child."

The man looked back, and said, *"No, but aren't they all our children?"*

Yes, they are all our children. They are also God's children, and He has entrusted us with their care, in Sarajevo, in Somalia, New York, Los Angeles, Oklahoma City, and in your town.

Jesus said, "I was hungry and you gave Me food; I was thirsty and you gave Me drink; I was a stranger and you took Me in; I was naked and you clothed Me; I was sick and you visited Me; I was in prison and you came to Me. . . . Assuredly, I say to you, inasmuch as you did it to one of the least of these My brethren, you did it to Me" (Matthew 25:35–40).

We must take these words to heart and become caring, giving people who are willing to reach out and love our children, and our neighbors, as ourselves.

I sought my soul, but my soul I could not see. I sought my God, but my God eluded me.
I sought my brother, and I found all three.
AUTHOR UNKNOWN

MALNUTRITION IS ASSOCIATED WITH OVER HALF
(FIFTY–FIVE PERCENT) OF ALL CHILD DEATHS THAT OCCUR
IN DEVELOPING COUNTRIES.
(UNICEF)

Am I My Brother's Keeper?

I n the first book of the Bible, Cain asked God, "Am I my brother's keeper?" We've had trouble answering that question ever since. The lawyer confronting Jesus just slightly rephrased Cain's question when he asked, "Who is my neighbor?" And two thousand years later, we still don't know who our neighbor is. We don't get it.

Nowadays, we live so fast that we don't even see the poor people around us, let alone get to know them. We don't go where the poor live. Most of us don't even know someone who lives in poverty. The Bible says "the Word [Jesus] became flesh and dwelt among us" (John 1:14); it doesn't say that Jesus came to dwell in a fancy apartment or a palatial home in the suburbs. Jesus lived among the poor. He even had to borrow a donkey for His triumphant entry into Jerusalem.

In contrast, most people today do their best to avoid the poor. We look the other way or talk with someone in the back seat when we stop at a traffic light and see a homeless person begging. We stay conveniently separated from the poor, living in our comfortable homes, eating far more food than most of us should. We enjoy our fresh new clothes, our expensive cars, boats, and other accoutrements that accompany the good life we've worked so hard to achieve. These material things aren't necessarily wrong, but we will never impress the poor with our homes, cars, boats, or Rolex watches. We can only impress them with our love. And to love them, you have to rub shoulders with poor people.

Former President Jimmy Carter shares a story in his book, *Living Faith*, about his Sunday school class in his home church. Around Thanksgiving one year, the class members wanted to make up food baskets to hand out to the poor and needy. They made up fifty beautiful baskets before discovering that they had a problem: Nobody in the class knew any poor people. Finally, the class members called their local office of the Department of Human Services and asked for some names of people whom they might help.

Jimmy Carter's story illustrates a key problem: We're church oriented, not neighbor oriented. We don't know their names or rub elbows with them. We bypass the poor and barely realize that they even exist. But Jesus knows them, and He says "as you did it to one of the least of these My brethren, you did it to Me" (Matthew 25:40). And conversely, "as you did not do it to one of the least of these, you did not do it to Me" (Matthew 25:45).

The way we treat our neighbor is the way we treat God.

Not My Job, Man!

I n the 1970s, a comedian named Freddie Prinz soared to fame on a television sitcom, *Chico and the Man*. One of Freddie's lines that always elicited a laugh (or at least a push of the laugh track button) was Freddie's slogan, "Not my job, man!" Unfortunately, many of us have adopted a similar attitude when it comes to helping hurting people.

In the story of the Good Samaritan, the traveler is beaten up and left for dead in the ditch beside the road. That was bad enough. But adding insult to injury is the fact that the two religious men see the victim in his need, and both consciously ignore him and pass by on the other side. Indeed, those who pass by today's hurting and needy are not on God's side; they are on the other side.

Lord, let my heart be broken by the things that break the heart of God.

BOB PIERCE, FOUNDER OF WORLD VISION

Christians need to pray, "Lord, let my heart be broken by the things that break the heart of God." If you truly have such a heart, you won't have to look very far to find someone who needs help. The ditch is full of people in pain.

You might be shocked to learn that one out of five children in the United States of America struggles with hunger every day. That equates to more than twelve million hungry children in a land where most of us are trying to lose weight. This country has nearly ten million single mothers struggling to make ends meet. We have nearly four million children who are being cared for by their grandparents. In some sections of our nation, one out of every three children is born into a home with an absentee father.

"But I thought our government welfare and public assistance programs take care of those individuals," many people say. "The government is doing it, so I don't have any responsibility. After all, I pay taxes. It's not my job to help."

Not so. According to a recent survey, nearly fifty percent of the people who have made it off welfare and found jobs are working as much as they can and still cannot feed their children.

Even in our church circles, we tend to think, "Let the pastor do it. Let the youth workers do it. Let the missionaries do that sort of work. I pay my tithes. Let somebody else take care of the poor."

One of the most often heard justifications for not being a good neighbor, nowadays, is something that the priest might have thought about the wounded man: "He made his own choice. Let him suffer the consequences." Certainly, there is some truth in that, and taking responsibility for mistakes is part of learning and maturing. But to hit somebody when they are already down is one of the cruelest things that we can do. Furthermore, those who are in the ditch are already paying for their mistakes. Let's help people who need help when they need it, and then maybe we will have earned the right to help them redirect their lives onto a better path.

The guy in the ditch is half–dead. He doesn't need a sermon; he needs help! But the priest decides that it's not his job.

The Levite comes along, and when he sees the man in the ditch, he perceives a problem rather than an opportunity. It's easy to imagine him thinking: "I can't get involved in this situation. I have places to go, and important things to do. I can't be interrupted."

Many of us today are so busy that if God Himself wanted to have an appointment with us, it would take three weeks to fit Him into our schedules. Our appointment books are full. We can't be interrupted. We're doing important work for the Kingdom.

Interesting, isn't it, that Jesus didn't feel that way. His greatest concern was always meeting people's needs. For instance, He was on his way to heal Jairus's daughter, when He was spotted by a woman who had been sick for twelve years. The woman pushed through the crowd, fell to her knees, touched the hem of Jesus' garment, and she was made well. Jesus was on His way to meet one human need when He met another human need. If we truly want to be like Jesus, we must let our lives be interrupted to meet human needs.

Another time, Jesus was getting ready to eat dinner at Peter's house, but first, He healed Peter's mother-in-law. On another occasion, Jesus was preaching, teaching, and healing when He allowed Himself to be interrupted by a guy being let down through the roof by several of his friends. Jesus didn't say, "Man, get in line. Other people were here before you. Can't you see I'm busy; my agenda is already full." No, Jesus healed the man and was impressed by the faith of the friends who brought him. Jesus put others' needs ahead of His own needs.

If you truly want to be like Jesus, let your life be interrupted to meet human needs.

Today, we talk a lot about meeting people's needs. We have conferences, conventions, and seminars about how we can meet human needs. We take surveys, and conduct polls about meeting human needs. We just don't do it!

You don't need a Ph.D. in meeting human needs if you really want to do it. All you need is a heart filled with a love like that of Jesus.

Many people do not want to know that we have hungry children in our country. They'd rather turn the channel than see a picture of a little boy or girl who is starving in this land of plenty, as if by changing the channel on their television set, the problem will miraculously go away. It won't. Approximately seventy-five percent of the hungry children we nourish through the work of Feed The Children are not in India, or Afghanistan, or some other poor Third World Country.

They're in the United States.

We are not born for ourselves.
MATTHEW HENRY

If we are not our brother's keeper let us at least not be his executioner.
MARLON BRANDO

Just Walk On By

The Levite was indifferent to the hurting man alongside the road. Maybe he'd seen too many hurting people before. Maybe he'd been ripped off by charlatans just trying to get a handout. Perhaps he'd passed too many "Will Work for Food" signs, knowing that when the offer of food was given, all too often the real request was for cash to purchase another bottle of beer or pack of cigarettes.

Pastor E. V. Hill once told me:

"You have to accept the fact that if you are going to feed hurting people, there will be a certain percentage of people who will try to rip you off. Their need is illegitimate, they may be running some sort of scam, or they may simply be lazy. But about seventy percent of the people who come to you will be destitute. They're not trying to beat the system; they need your help. Sure, thirty percent are trying to get something for nothing, so just accept that. Some are liars and cheats, but that's not your concern. Let God take care of them. If you spend your time trying to divide out who is really needy and who is not, you'll waste most of your time, and you'll probably miss a lot of needy people. Let God do the dividing."

Of course, at Feed The Children, we do everything in our power to make sure we are meeting legitimate needs, that we are being good stewards of the resources God puts in our hands to be distributed to hurting people. No doubt, there are times when we get ripped off, but that does not justify us ignoring human need.

> *There is a thing that is worse than evil. What is it? It is indifference to evil.*
> ELIE WIESEL, HOLOCAUST SURVIVOR
> WINNER OF THE NOBEL PEACE PRIZE

Too many people follow the path of least assistance.
ANONYMOUS

Give me the ready hand rather than the ready tongue.
GIUSEPPE GARIBALDI

How do you keep from becoming hard and insensitive to hurting people? It happens. After a while, you tire of hearing, "I need money because my grandmother died and I want to go to the funeral." You know even as you listen to the story that the same grandmother has "died" around twenty times this month. It's the one of the oldest stories in the books. Certainly, though, some people do have genuine needs, and if we can verify the need, we will try to help.

But if you want to be a good neighbor and do the work of God in our world, you must keep your heart soft and sensitive. We dare not forget where we came from, that Jesus rescued each of us out of a ditch of some kind. Now, we are simply doing for others what He has done for us.

The tragedy of man is that he dies inside while he is still alive. Science may have found a cure for most evils; but it has found no remedy for the worst of them all—the apathy of human beings.
Helen Keller

When it comes to personally dealing with society's diseases, we are often like the man who got so upset seeing the newspaper articles about the guns and shootings in his neighborhood that he knew he had to do something—so he canceled his newspaper subscription.

Apathy avoids, empathy embraces; indifference ignores; compassion cares. Love is a verb.

It's often been said that a good minister is one who comforts the afflicted and afflicts the comfortable. Unfortunately, when it comes to helping the needy, many of us don't want to be afflicted.

Julius Caesar said, "I came, I saw, I conquered." Many of us are like the priest and the Levite in Jesus' story. We say, "I came, I saw, I walked away."

Love me or hate me, but spare me your indifference.
LIBBIE FUDIM

You'll never plow a field by turning it over in your mind.
IRISH PROVERB

Jesus in Disguise

"The dying, the crippled, the mentally ill, the unwanted, the unloved—they are Jesus in disguise."

MOTHER TERESA

Mother Teresa, the compassionate nun known for her work in the squalor of Calcutta, once said, "Sometimes Jesus comes to us in the most disgusting disguise that we don't recognize Him." I'll never forget when I visited with Mother Teresa's sister ministry, Missionaries of Charity, in Ethiopia. I was overwhelmed by the horrendous poverty and the awful need.

At the end of my first day there, the sisters asked me, "Would you like to come back in the morning and help pull people out of the ditch with us?"

"What do you mean?" I asked.

"Every morning at the back gates, the poor people come, and they sleep in the ditch. In the morning, we go out and get them, and bring them in, and put them in a clinic."

Not really sure what I was volunteering for, I said, "Yes, I would like to do that. We'll be here in the morning at about quarter till seven."

Through our work with Feed The Children, I thought that I had seen every sort of poverty and starvation, but I was unprepared for what I saw the following morning. When the nuns opened the gates, I found fifteen older men and women lying in the ditch alongside the street. These older people, whose children can no longer care for them, seek help from the nuns when they sense they are about to die. Many of the people in the ditch had not bathed in months, and the stench was one of the worst I had ever smelled. Dirt and filth were caked on their skin and layers of tattered clothes.

At first, as I reached out to pick these people up, I worried that I would hurt them. They were extremely thin, and I thought that if I squeezed just a little too hard, their brittle bones would shatter. They could hardly walk. Most had to be carried.

I carried them into the clinic where the nuns offered what little assistance, medical attention, and food they could. I thought, "This is so far removed from where most of us 'good church folks' live. This is the real ministry that we all talk about but never seem to get around to doing."

As I watched the tender care those sisters gave to each poor, dying soul, I felt so ashamed. I was over forty years old, and that was the first time I had ever helped someone out of a ditch. Even though these people were dying, the sisters treated each person with love and respect. It was one of the most powerful sermons I've ever experienced. Those Sisters were bringing people out of the ditch, into their home, and caring for them, knowing full well that they were probably going to die—but they would die knowing that somebody loves them, especially God.

And they did it again and again, every morning.

There in that squalor of Ethiopia, I found Jesus disguised. I've also found Him disguised as street children in Romania, as AIDS victims in Kenya, and as the children in the garbage dump in Manila. Once you see Jesus in the poor and the needy, you are never the same.

Once you see Jesus in the poor and the needy, you are never the same.

I know that many people—even good, compassionate people—are extremely uncomfortable when confronted with the very needy. I wasn't fearful when I started pulling people from the ditch that day; I just didn't know how to do it. But I soon discovered that I didn't have to know very much; I just needed to be there.

No doubt, there are dangers. The poor of the world don't always meet our standards of civility or sanitation. I'm sure that many of the people I picked up that morning had lice. After I left there, I felt itchy all day long. And I could not get that awful, putrid stench out of my nostrils.

But when we look into the eyes of that poor person, we are reminded Christ died for him every bit as much as He died for us. And Jesus says, "If you have done it unto one of the least of these, you have done it unto me." That is where you meet Christ in disguise.

> When a poor person dies of hunger, it has not happened because God did not take care of him or her.
> It has happened because neither you nor I wanted to give that person what he or she needed....
> It has happened because we did not recognize Christ when, once more,
> He appeared under the guise of pain.
> MOTHER TERESA

EIGHTY-SEVEN DEVELOPING COUNTRIES
DO NOT PRODUCE ENOUGH FOOD FOR THEIR PEOPLE
AND CANNOT AFFORD TO IMPORT THE REST.
(FOOD AND AGRICULTURE ORGANIZATION OF THE UNITED NATIONS)

Echoes from the Ditch

Two years after my encounter with little nine-year-old Jerry in Haiti, I returned to that country to oversee some of the relief efforts Feed The Children had begun. While there, I participated in an area–wide pastors' conference in which an American speaker brought a stirring message on "The Miracle of Jesus Feeding the Multitude," based on Mark 6:35–43. You probably recall the account of the little boy who brought his five loaves and two fishes to Jesus, and Jesus fed more than five thousand people with that little bit. Amazing, isn't it?

But what if that hillside supper had ended differently? The little boy could have slipped behind a tree and had his lunch all to himself. But he didn't. He gave what he had to Jesus. The Lord blessed it, broke it, and gave it to His disciples, and they distributed the food to the throng of people.

At other points in the story, this miracle also could have broken down. What if Jesus had decided to eat the lunch Himself? What if the disciples, who were certainly hungry, had said, "Hey, there's just enough for a bite or two for each of us. We could never feed this many people, so we might as well take care of ourselves."

In fact, the miracle almost was thwarted when Andrew, one of the disciples, took a look at the five loaves and two fish and said, "But what good is that with this huge crowd?" (John 6:9, NLT)

Many modern Christians have adopted that same attitude. Focusing on what they have, they say, "This is all we've got." But Jesus knows what He can do with even a little bit. In the story, Jesus didn't tell the people to go home; instead, He said, "Tell the folks to sit down. It's dinner time."

The miracle took place because somebody gave away what had been given to him.

The miracle took place because at each point along the way somebody gave away what had been given to him. That was the lesson I learned from that pastors' conference. During a question and answer session after the American pastor's message, a Haitian pastor stood up and asked politely, "What would have happened had Jesus' disciples taken the loaves and fishes and gone over, sat down under a tree, and eaten all the food themselves?"

I was so glad that I wasn't sitting on the platform that day because I knew what the Haitian pastor was implying. He wondered, "How can the people of the United States, blessed with a wealth of resources, call themselves a Christian nation, and yet turn their backs and be so indifferent to the poverty of countries just a few hundred miles to the south?"

After all, the United States has more than five loaves and two fish. It owns the fish pond, the farm, and the bakery! Instead of blessing others in need, we have taken the resources God has given to us and hoarded them for ourselves. Yet God works miracles through those of us who are willing to place even our "little" into His hands.

Much of what God can accomplish in and through our lives depends on our attitudes. It's interesting to compare our attitude to those displayed in the story of the Good Samaritan.

The Robbers' Attitude—Greed: "What's mine is mine, and what's yours is mine if I can get it."

The Priest and Levite's Attitude—Selfishness: "What's mine is mine, and what's yours is yours if you can keep it."

The Samaritan's Attitude—Christ-like: "What's yours is yours, and what's mine is yours if you need it."

What If Your Church Closed Its Doors?

J esus said that His followers should be like salt and light in the world (Matt. 5:13–14). Salt makes people thirsty for the gospel and serves as a purifying agent. Light shines in the darkness, showing people the way to safety. We, as the church, too often have failed to act as the salt and the light in our world. When Christians fail to live out their faith, then our families fail to function as Christian families. Failed Christian families make ineffective churches, and ineffective churches make no impact on the communities they have been called to serve and change.

At another pastors' conference, the speaker asked a tough question: "If your church closed its doors tomorrow, would it have a negative impact on your community? Not on just you, but on the community—would they notice?"

You can find a church building on nearly every corner in America, but our communities are being systematically destroyed by violence as people languish in poverty and despair. It is obvious that the church is not having the influence that God intends it to have. When people are hurting physically, it doesn't take long before they lose hope spiritually. On the other hand, if we meet their basic needs for food, clothing, and shelter, the door opens to point them to Christ. Many times people have come to me and said, "I want to thank you for the box of food your group gave to me, but it means even more to me that you know that this food gives me hope."

If your church closed its doors tomorrow, would it have a negative impact on your community?

It is easy enough to tell the poor to accept their poverty as God's will when you yourself have warm clothes and plenty of food and medical care and a roof over your head and no worry about the rent. But if you want them to believe you . . . try to share some of their poverty and see if you can accept it as God's will yourself!

THOMAS MERTON

Rich Ditch or Poor Ditch—It's Still a Ditch

Years ago Father John Powell told the story of Norma Jean Mortenson. Her mother periodically was committed to a mental institution, and Norma Jean spent much of her childhood in foster homes. When she was eight years old, one of the boarders at a foster home raped her, then gave her a nickel. He said, "Here, Honey. Take this, and don't ever tell anyone what I did to you."

When Norma Jean confided to her foster mother what had happened, she was beaten badly. She was told, "Our boarder pays good rent. Don't you ever say anything bad about him!" At the age of eight, she was told that she had no value. Norma Jean grew to be a very pretty young girl, and people began to notice her. But she wished they would notice she was a person too—not just a body or a pretty face, but a person.

You probably recall the story how Norma Jean went to Hollywood and took a new name—Marilyn Monroe. She was a huge success, but she kept asking, "Did you also notice I am a person? Would you please notice?"

Often, she kept her crews waiting two hours on the set. She was regarded as a selfish prima donna. What they didn't know was that she was in her dressing room vomiting because she was so terrified. She kept saying, "Will someone please notice I am a person? Please!"

But they didn't.

She went through three marriages—always pleading, "Take me seriously as a person." People around her said, "But you are a sex symbol. You can't be anything other than that." And Marilyn protested, "I want to be a person. I want to be a serious actress."

At the age of thirty-five, Marilyn Monroe took her own life. When her maid found her body the next morning, she noticed the telephone was off the hook, dangling beside the dead body of the star. An investigation revealed that in the last moments of her life, she had called a Hollywood actor and told him she had taken enough sleeping pills to kill herself.

He answered with the crude, famous line of Rhett Butler. Those were the last words Norma Jean Mortenson ever heard. Then she dropped the phone—and left it dangling.

Claire Booth Luce, in a sensitive article, suggested that the dangling telephone was the symbol of Marilyn Monroe's whole life. She died because she never got through to anyone who understood—or cared.

The worst part of living in the ditch is the feeling that nobody cares, nobody identifies with the pain and the awful loneliness. It's a sense of being unwanted that is more painful than what originally put the person in the ditch.

Mother Teresa once told an interviewer:

"In these years of work among the people, I have come more and more to realize that it is being unwanted that is the worst disease any human being can ever experience. Nowadays, we have found medicine for leprosy and lepers can be cured. For all kinds of diseases there are medicines and cures. But as for being unwanted, unless there are willing hands to serve and there's a loving heart to love, I don't think this terrible disease can ever be cured."

Mother Teresa was right. If we are ever going to help people who are in life's ditches, we must first care that they are there. The people in the ditch don't care how much we know, until they know how much we care.

We must learn to regard people less in the light of what they do or omit to do, and more in the light of what they suffer.
DIETRICH BONHOEFFER

The Wounded
Won't Wait

———

Then Jesus said, "Which one of these three men do you think was a neighbor to the man who was attacked by the robbers?" The expert on the law answered, "The one who showed him mercy."

The Need is Now

In 1984, I led a team of Feed The Children staff to Ethiopia to assess the needs of that country. At the time, Ethiopia was in the throes of a terrible drought and famine.

We arrived during Thanksgiving week and went to the small village of Bati. On Thanksgiving Day, we learned that 67 people had died. The next day 74 more died, the next day 87, and the next day 91. Every minute we were there, the famine grew worse. Every hour the horrifying statistics rose.

A refugee camp had been set up in the village. Three thousand starving people were expected, but a full eighteen thousand soon crowded into the village. Clean water and food were scarce. Cholera and dysentery ran rampant. The facilities for disposal of garbage and waste were almost non-existent. Medical attention was crude and inadequate.

Before long, a section of the makeshift hospital was dubbed the "Ward Nearest Heaven." Into this ward poured people for whom there was little hope of living much longer. Their bodies, having succumbed to the ravages of starvation and disease, were feeding off themselves. Before that drought and famine in Ethiopia relented, more than one million refugees died in a similar manner.

As I witnessed the pain of stark reality, one particular little boy haunted me: Ali Hassein, a wisp of a ten-year-old who looked to be more like he was five. He had traveled many days with his father to reach the refugee camp, their last hope for help. His grandmother had been left behind at home to die, being too ill even to attempt crossing the barren terrain. Ali's sisters had not survived the trek.

There in the tent I held Ali's shivering body, and I later prayed for him during the night. To my astonishment, Ali was still alive when I returned in the morning, his will to keep breathing just a bit stronger than his failing body. Doctors told me, however, that it didn't look good for this small child. Hunger and hardship had taken their toll. As I turned to check on the next guest, I heard a gasp—I quickly turned around and saw that Ali had just taken his last breath.

Another pleading prayer, another passionate hug, another kiss from his father, and little Ali was gone. Just one of millions who never had a chance to blossom and grow. He was one of God's precious children who left a hole in my heart, a hole that will never be filled until every hungry child on the face of this earth is fed and loved.

I'll also never forget the Saturday when the Lord used a tiny baby girl to rearrange my priorities.

When my wife, Frances, and I travel overseas, our schedule is always tight. On this particular day, our itinerary had been carefully

No one need wait a single moment before starting to improve the world.
ANNE FRANK

arranged, every moment and every person accounted for. We were staying in Addis Ababa, the capital of Ethiopia, and planned to make a four-hour journey to Enemor, where we had arranged to film a family for our television program.

As we drove up to our compound in Enemor, people were lined up, waiting for us. When the gate swung open, a woman shoved to the front of the crowd. Cradled in her arms was one of the tiniest human babies I've ever seen. "Help me. Please help me," her eyes desperately pleaded, as she held that little body up to the car window.

It didn't take much to see that the baby girl was extremely sick.

"We've got to do something," Frances said urgently.

I agreed. "We'll get her some food right away."

Feed The Children had a warehouse inside the Enemor compound, so we went inside and found some powdered milk, gave it to the baby's mother, then set out for our meeting with the prearranged family. I didn't realize it yet, but God was trying to tell me something. God tried again when we arrived at the family's hut and again saw the desperate mother and her tiny baby, but we did our filming and returned to Addis Ababa.

But as I sat in the stillness of the evening after our hectic day, I couldn't get that little girl out of my mind. She needed more than food; she needed medical attention, too.

Thoughts of past sermons crowded into my mind. What had I said? I recalled preaching that many of Christ's miracles occurred because He was willing to let people interrupt Him. I recalled saying that although Christ didn't heal or feed everyone who lived during His earthly ministry, He always helped those who came within the scope of His awareness. Now those sermons were preaching at me.

"Frances," I said, "we've got to go back to Enemor."

"But how can we?" she replied. "We're supposed to leave tomorrow for Kenya. We can't be in two places at once."

"I'm going back to find that baby," I said quietly. "I'll rearrange my entire schedule if I have to."

The following day, Frances and the television crew continued on to Kenya as planned. I took part of our team and drove back to Enemor. We didn't have to search long to find the woman and her daughter. We took them immediately to a hospital, where we learned that the little girl, named Zeru, was actually a one-year-old child but weighed only six pounds. If she had had to wait any longer for help, she surely would have died.

Doctors and nurses assured us they could nurse Zeru to a semblance of health if we would leave her and her mother there for thirty days. We covered the cost of care; Zeru would be treated and her mother would receive food during her daughter's hospitalization. The bill amounted to only $2 a day—a pitifully small amount to have made such a difference.

In the story of the Good Samaritan, I don't think it was coincidental that two of the passers-by were religious people who left the man bleeding in the ditch. A religious person myself, I almost did the same with little Zeru.

When I got back to the States, I met with my staff and told them about Zeru. I confessed to them that sometimes we're so busy with our own schedules and with all the things we think we "have to do," that we fail to see the things that God needs us to do. I don't ever want to miss another "Zeru."

The Zeru in your life may look like one of life's interruptions, but it may just be one of God's opportunities for you.

The wounded, hurting, beaten, battered, and sick will come alive if we love them enough. Your first thought when you see your

You cannot do a kindness too soon, for you never know how soon it will be too late.
RALPH WALDO EMERSON

neighbor in need can start a miracle or kill a miracle.

Remember, the wounded won't wait. They demand our full attention. We need to care about others as surely as we need to breathe. We need to recognize the opportunity and accept the responsibility. We need to be like Jesus.

Although great occasions to reach out may seldom come our way, small occasions surround us on a daily basis. We must become a body of caring people who see the problem and become the answer. We don't live in a vacuum, in a world of our own. Our brothers and sisters live here, too. It's not our ability that God wants, but our availability. People who make a difference are not ones with credentials, but ones with concern.

On every street corner, there is work to be done. In every community, there are wounds to heal. And in every heart, there is the power to do it. What we accomplish for our neighbor may just be the thing God needs to accomplish. Remember, "we are ambassadors for Christ, as though God were pleading through us" (2 Corinthians 5:20).

It's not our ability that God wants, but our availability.

In the eternal scheme of things, you will find that the moments that really stand out—the redeeming moments when you truly live, when you receive an abundance of outer joy and inner peace—are when you reach across the fences and help a "neighbor" in need.

So go ahead. Let God interrupt your life. It just might be the opportunity and the occasion for Him to do His work through you. In the eternal scheme of things, nothing else matters.

Love Will Find a Way

When I started traveling overseas, I quickly learned something important from another religion: The Muslims don't go to hurting people with an evangelistic crusade as Americans tend to do. They go to the poorest part of town and build a clinic. Next to the clinic, they build a school, then they build a mosque. The day the building's doors open, it is full. Americans go in, and—I call it beating on a telephone pole with a Bible—tell everyone that they are going to hell. Which method do you think is more effective? Christians need to understand that if we want to have a hearing with the world today, we must meet human need.

While Americans have done an admirable job of cursing the darkness, we have done a poor job of spreading the light.

Most of the evangelistic efforts sponsored by Americans still put more money into a crusade, rather than meeting human needs. Certainly, many mission organizations and Christian–based humanitarian organizations are doing a wonderful job, but others are doing more along this line than we are.

Many Christians are extremely reticent to use the word "social" with the gospel, but the gospel always brings social responsibility. Jesus called it loving your neighbor.

Kindness is a language that the deaf can hear and the blind can see.
MARK TWAIN

The Gift of a Mother

M any years ago in a small town in northern Arkansas, a young mother named Effie Hackler fought desperately to keep alive her critically ill infant, Barbara Ann. After a six–week struggle, Effie lost that battle.

The heartache of losing Barbara Ann was unbearable. Yet, even though Effie's despair ran deep and her thoughts remained troubled, just days after the funeral, she was asked to make one of the most difficult decisions of her life.

The local physician, Dr. Gray, came to the door one evening while Effie was still grieving her loss. He had a request to make. A young mother just down the road had given birth recently. "The baby is quite sick," the doctor said, "and the mother is unable to produce any breast milk to feed him. Attempts to feed the little boy goat's milk and cow's milk have failed. The situation is grave."

Then Dr. Gray looked at Effie and made this astonishing request: "Will you nurse this tiny baby as your own and give him a chance at life?"

Pain seared Effie's heart. Would she have the strength to watch another baby nurse at the same breast that only days earlier had nursed her own ailing baby? Could she put aside her loss and offer herself to another? Could she nourish and nurture another woman's child?

Dr. Gray came back the next morning. Effie looked directly into his eyes, her decision made after a sleepless night. "Yes. I will do it," she whispered. "I'll nurse my neighbor's newborn baby." Her decision was an unselfish testimonial to the compassion and love that God reserves especially for mothers.

The first time Effie put the little one to her breast, her heart ached like ripping a wound that had not even begun to heal. But Effie quickly discovered that the newborn did not take anything away from her. Rather, the child brought comfort to her.

"As I watched the baby flourish and grow from the nourishment I provided," Effie later said, "I began to feel nourished myself. The nursing process quickened my healing process, and I handled my grief better each time the baby came to me."

Effie nursed that little boy for weeks, morning, noon, and night—long enough for him to overcome his illness and get a healthy start in life.

Years later, this story was related to me by my wife, Frances, who had heard the story from Effie Hackler herself—my wife's mother.

Charity is a naked child giving honey to a bee without wings.
FRANCIS QUARLES

Love is not blind. Love is the only thing that sees.
FRANK CRANE

Do all the good you can.
By all the means you can.
In all the ways you can.
In all the places you can.
At all the times you can.
To all the people you can.
As long as ever you can.

JOHN WESLEY

How much we are willing to sacrifice
is a measure of our love.

ANONYMOUS

Looking Need in the Face

I t's one thing to hear about human need; it's another thing to see it. When need has a face, it somehow becomes more personal. For instance, the encounter with young Jerry in Haiti back in 1979 made me vitally aware of the community's overwhelming poverty, and the result of that awareness is the Feed The Children ministry.

Even if you haven't seen intense human need in person, you might have seen it on television. Maybe you've even caught the award-winning, weekly television humanitarian documentary Larry Jones Presents / FEED THE CHILDREN. The nationally syndicated program illustrates the devastating effects of hunger and provides opportunities to help.

On the following pages of this book, you'll see the faces of many people—some well-known, some anonymous; some in need, some lending a hand; some on the other side of the world, some maybe in your own city. What do they all have in common? Each one is dearly loved and uniquely created. Look at the faces and try to see their Creator in them.

Friends & Inspiration

Larry and Frances Jones walk through a village in Kibera, near Nairobi, Kenya. The couple is a true team in Feed The Children, and Frances' efforts have been recognized internationally. In April 2002, the STAR Group honored her as one of the forty Leading Women Entrepreneurs of the World—the first time someone from a charity was named to the prestigious list.

Mother Teresa's example has been an inspiration to Larry Jones and others who see "Jesus in disguise" in the poor. Larry worked with Mother Teresa after the 1988 Armenia earthquake.

It's all about children. Marija Topalovic—at right with Larry Jones, Frances, and Oklahoma Congressman J. C. Watts—first entered Larry and Frances' lives in a makeshift Bosnian hospital. She had lost both legs in an explosion that also killed her father, during the war in Bosnia. Larry and Frances brought her to the U.S. where she was cared for and fitted for prosthetics. Now she's a strong young woman determined to live life to the fullest.

Helping Families in the U.S.

Crowds gather in Harlem for another massive food distribution.

Trucks line up for blocks in Washington Heights, an inner-city neighborhood of New York, on Sept. 9, 2001. A few days later, Feed The Children turned its efforts toward helping in the aftermath of the World Trade Center attacks

A food distribution in Los Angeles is a hive of activity.

STAR Touring and Riding Association, a motorcyclists' group, helped at a food distribution in Bowling Green, Kentucky. Many delivered food on their bikes.

The United States is proud of being the richest country on earth, but thousands of U. S. children still go to bed hungry. Feed The Children invests more than half of its efforts in American neighborhoods and families.

Congressman Charles Rangel and Larry Jones talk amid the buzz of activity during a Harlem food distribution in December 2001.

The mission of Feed The Children gets attention from the highest reaches of world governments, including U. S. presidents like Ronald Reagan.

Who's your neighbor? The man who unloads a truck full of food and supplies that you need.

Senator Hillary Clinton helps distribute food with Larry Jones in Harlem in December 2001.

Helping Families in the U.S.

Feed The Children delivers more than food. In this Dallas food distribution, Larry Jones hands children one of the most basic health tools—a toothbrush.

You never know who's going to show up. Bishop T. D. Jakes and football star Emmitt Smith joined Larry and Frances Jones as they helped distribute boxes in Dallas.

Larry Jones walks through a makeshift tent community assembled in the aftermath of Hurricane Andrew, which slammed into South Florida in August 1992. It was the costliest natural disaster in U. S. history.

Larry and Frances Jones were in New York on the day the World Trade Center was attacked. Feed the Children was therefore able to jumpstart the delivery of food and rescue items to the affected area.

Friends in Ministries

Matt and Laurie Crouch, who work with Trinity Broadcasting Network, came out to support Feed The Children at a Los Angeles food distribution.

The Rev. R. W. Shambaugh talks with Larry Jones at a food distribution.

Larry Jones elaborates on the work of Feed The Children while talking with Benny Hinn.

Dr. Kenneth C. Ulmer, Bishop of Faithful Central Bible Church in Inglewood, California, greets Larry Jones at a food distribution in April 2001.

Actress Melanie Griffith saw a Feed The Children program on television one night, and she immediately volunteered to help, even bringing Planet Hollywood restaurants into the effort.

"You think that it's not in your neighborhood. You don't see it in your neighborhood. But just hear the statistics— one in every four children in America is starving. That's scary. And this is America; it's not supposed to be here."

—MELANIE GRIFFITH

Actor, musician, and writer Kris Kristofferson greets Frances Jones at a food distribution.

Geraldo Rivera and Larry Jones talk about the urgent mission of Feed The Children.

Actress Melanie Griffith brought her husband, actor Antonio Banderas, and her mother, actress Tippi Hedrin, to a food distribution.

Actress Laurie Holden joins Larry and Frances Jones at a food distribution.

Larry Jones stands with actresses Mindy Sterling and Bobby Eakes at a food distribution.

Actor Gavin McLeod totes food with Larry Jones.

Larry and Frances Jones often present Feed The Children trucks to supporters like actor John Ritter.

Comedian Sinbad greets Larry and Frances Jones at a charity event.

The New York Jets lend their muscles to unloading a
truck during a Harlem food drop.

Deion Sanders is a power-player off the football field, too,
as he helps organizations like Feed The Children.

Michael Chang helped
Feed The Children
deliver 308,000
pounds of food to the
needy in South Florida
before a tennis match
there. The Lipton Food
Company donated the
food, which was then
distributed by seventy-
eight local agencies.

Butch Buccholz, tournament chairman, and
tennis greats Jennifer Capriati and Alex
Corretja join Larry and Frances Jones at the
site of the Ericsson Open Tennis Tournament
in Key Biscayne, Florida. Feed The Children
distributed twelve truckloads of food to sixty
of South Florida's hunger relief agencies at
the March, 2001 event.

Football standout Emmitt Smith has supported
several food distributions by Feed The Children.

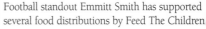

Chris Evert and Tracy Austin were among the sports stars who shined support on a food distribution at the Boca Raton campus of Florida Atlantic University in February 2000.

he racing team of John Hollansworth, Jr., helped Feed he Children collect 30,000 pounds of food at Texas Motor Speedway in 1999. The truckful of donations as given to a local food bank, which used it to fill their mergency distribution needs.

Coach Henry Bibby and his USC Trojans basketball team listen as Larry Jones explains how to help at a food distribution.

Former Texas Ranger John Wetteland and his wife, Michelle, launched annual toy drives for Feed The Children, and their example has spread to other ball clubs.

FEED THE CHIL

Friends

The Oak Ridge Boys pose with the Harlem Boys and Girls Choir.

I think one of the reasons we decided to get involved with Larry Jones is because he impressed us from d one. His organization gives right to where the need That's one of the reasons the Oak Ridge Boys wante to get involved almost twenty years ago, and we're still very glad we are involved with him even today. ...The job is a tremendous job that needs to be done It's bigger than any of us, but it's not bigger than all us together.

—RICHARD STERBAN, OAK RIDGE BC

The Oak Ridge Boys help unload a truck in Harlem. Their support of Feed The Children over the years has included raising money to dig wells for villages in Africa.

Violinist Boyd Tinsley, a member of the Dave Matthews Band, joined Larry Jones in overseeing a food distribution in Salt Lake City, Utah.

Country star Tim McGraw sings for children's supper.

Larry and Frances Jones present singer Wayne Newton with a truck in thanks for his support.

in Music

Members of the band Jars of Clay join Larry Jones at a New Orleans food distribution.

Gospel singer Andrae Crouch speaks up for Feed The Children.

Carman accompanied Larry and Frances Jones on a trip to impoverished communities in Africa.

Members of the group Avalon help out at a work site.

Anita Bryant receives a Feed The Children truck from Larry and Frances Jones in thanks for her support.

Singer Pam Tillis and Frances Jones take a break in a warehouse filled with supplies for a Feed The Children distribution.

Musician Jermaine Jackson came to support the grand opening of the first Frances Jones Abandoned Baby Center in Kenya. He is the founder, chairman, and CEO of EarthCare International, a non-profit organization committed to using its resources to help improve the health of people in developing countries.

Singer Carman visits Larry and Frances Jones at the Frances Jones Abandoned Baby Center in Kenya. Feed The Children plans to open several Abandoned Baby Centers to nurture babies who are discarded or orphaned by families ravaged in the HIV/AIDS epidemic.

Frances Jones holds young Susan Awino while Larry Jones displays the child's HIV-negative certificate after being HIV positive at birth.

©DGF

In 1979, a Haitian boy interrupted Larry Jones' life. The work of feeding children in that impoverished nation continues today.

Larry and Frances Jones tour an area of El Salvador destroyed by earthquakes in 2001.

rances Jones visits a family in El Salvador. More
an 300,000 people were left homeless by the
arthquakes and the resulting mudslides.

Feed The Children provided emergency relief in El Salvador after major earthquakes struck the Central American country early in 2001.

Helping Families

Feed The Children often offers educational support for people like these Romanian children.

Feed The Children makes a huge difference in villages like Tegu.

©DGF

Larry Jones walks with a resident of Dagoretti Children's Center in Nairobi. Before the AIDS epidemic, about two percent of children in developing countries were orphans, but now, in many hard-hit African countries, that figure has risen to ten percent.

Larry holds a Romanian boy who's being helped by Feed The Children.

Every child is precious, but love must "wear work clothes" if it's to fill hungry bellies.

Around the World

Political upheaval in countries like Angola continually threatens the ability for groups like Feed The Children to reach the needy.

©DGF

©DGF

Larry displays a bowl and pitcher representing the amount of maize and oil a family in Sierra Leone must live on for 30 days.

Jermaine Jackson scoops food onto plates for hungry families in Kibera near Nairobi, Kenya.

©DGF

After their parents die of AIDS-related complications, thousands of children have nowhere to go except streets like these. Pictured here are Larry Jones and Mike Espy, former Secretary of Agriculture.

©DGF

Larry Jones visits with a child in Kibera near Nairobi, Kenya. An estimated 50,000 children in Kibera have been orphaned by AIDS.

Helping Families in Afghanistan

More than six million people were displaced in Afghanistan in the wake of the Taliban's rule. Feed The Children quickly went to work in the Maslakh Internally Displaced Persons Camp—the single largest refugee camp in the world—to provide emergency food and shelter. Recovery efforts in the war-torn region are expected to take years.

©DGF

©DGF

Afghanistan, Dec. 2001—Larry Jones, delivering more than forty tons of food and relief supplies to Maslakh Internally Displaced Persons Camp in Herat.

Afghanistan, Dec. 2001—Larry Jones holds a hungry, barefoot Afghan child.

©DGF

Afghanistan, Dec. 2001—Larry Jones walks with two of the Afghan children, many of whom must go barefoot against the bitter cold.

Afghanistan, Dec. 2001—An Afghan mother and three children use a hole in the ground for shelter against the harsh cold.

The vocation of every man and woman
is to serve other people.

LEO TOLSTOY

Did you see Jesus in the preceding pictures? Did you see people's need of Him? Did you see your own need to help others fulfill their destinies in Him? The needs are there, waiting.

Tell me how much you know of the sufferings
of your fellow men and I will tell you
how much you have loved them.

HELMUT THIELICKE

Going the Second Mile

There are no traffic jams on the second mile.
ANONYMOUS

Under Roman law during biblical times, a soldier had the right to ask any Jewish citizen at any time to carry his backpack for one mile. A loaded military pack might weigh as much as seventy pounds, so carrying this burden often fueled resentment in the Jews who lived under the iron rule of the Romans. It was against this backdrop that Jesus commanded, "And whoever compels you to go one mile, go with him two" (Matthew 5:41).

The Good Samaritan went far beyond the second mile when he helped the man who had been beaten and left for dead. The Samaritan:

> pulled him out of the ditch,
> took him back to the inn,
> interrupted his own schedule,
> spent the night at the inn with the wounded man,
> left money in case he needed anything else,
> promised to return and pay any further expenses.

The Samaritan went not only the second mile, but the third, fourth, fifth and more. Love doesn't stop!

Robert Frost once said, "Pressed into service means pressed out of shape." We need a new definition of what it means to live disciplined Christian lives. Most of us think a good discipline is to spend thirty minutes with God every morning. Many Christians don't even do that well. There is much to learn, however, from the "discipline of being interrupted."

Nowadays, we hear outstanding speakers who motivate us to manage our time better, and we've bought into the idea that we must focus on our goals and not allow anything or anyone to divert us from accomplishing our plans. Rather than embracing interruptions, we do all that we can to avoid them.

But if we are going to go the second mile, if we truly hope to emulate the Good Samaritan, and in doing so, emulate Jesus, we must make allowances for interruptions. Otherwise we will miss God's opportunities.

The wounded man in the ditch needed emergency care, but the Samaritan didn't merely pull him out and then move on to the next crisis; he provided more substantial aid. Perhaps the Samaritan could easily have kept on and made his destination before dark, had he not allowed himself to be interrupted by the wounded man. If we are going to be second mile Christians, we must learn to be interrupted—and not be upset about it.

Everybody can be great. Because anybody can serve. You don't have to have a college degree to serve. You don't have to make your subject and your verb agree to serve. You don't have to know Einstein's theory of relativity to serve. You only need a heart full of grace. A soul generated by love.
MARTIN LUTHER KING, JR.

No one is useless in this world who lightens the burdens of anyone else.
CHARLES DICKENS

There are two kinds of persons in the world, those who think first of difficulties, and those who think first of the importance of accomplishment in spite of the difficulties.

Samuel Warren

The Circle of Suffering

Compassion is what makes a person feel pain when somebody else hurts.
ANONYMOUS

When Jesus met someone, He entered their circle of suffering, and ministered to them right where they were. Consider the leper who was made whole by Jesus or the disciples who feared for their lives as a storm tossed their boat on the Sea of Galilee. Jesus healed that leper, and He calmed the wind and the sea.

Nowadays, a popular phrase is "keep out of my space." Yet that is exactly what Jesus refused to do. He purposely entered people's space; He got involved in their lives, and wouldn't leave until the need was met.

From the story He told regarding the Good Samaritan, it is clear that He expects nothing less from us. When a person with a need comes into the scope of our awareness, we should move to meet that need.

Frankly, that means more than simply writing a check around the holiday season. We are programmed to be generous during Thanksgiving and Christmas. That is wonderful, but what about the rest of the year? Hunger doesn't take a vacation. Often, I tell people to whom Feed The Children delivers food, "The reason we are here in your town delivering food in August is because it isn't Christmas."

Moreover, it's easier to write a check than it is to enter somebody's circle of suffering and get personally involved with that individual or family. No doubt, the Good Samaritan could easily have written a check to the man in the ditch, and said, "I have a very full schedule, but here, my friend. Take this check and find yourself some help . . . if you make it." The government throws money at the problem of

Hunger doesn't take a vacation.

the poor, and sometimes so does the church. But God didn't send a check to save us. He sent His Son. He entered into our circle to save us, to deliver us from evil, and to heal us. Now He wants us to enter somebody else's circle of suffering to help them find life.

"Here is this little woman, who doesn't want a thing, never asked for anything for herself, never demanded anything, or shook her fist in anger, here's real power. It was a paradox. She has reached down into the gutter and loved and given. She has loved those the world sees as unlovable—the desolate, the dying—because they are created in the image of the God she serves."

Dee Jepsen, about Mother Teresa, who appeared in Washington, D.C. to attend a Capitol Hill luncheon in her honor

The loneliest place in the world is the human heart when love is absent.

Anonymous

*Let us not look back in anger
or forward in fear
but around in awareness.*

JAMES THURBER

No Hands But Yours

A church in Poland was bombed during the Second World War. In the explosion, a huge statue of Christ which was outside the front of the church was mutilated and the hands were blown off. The statue has not been restored. It stands there today with hands missing, but at the foot of the statue, these words have been inscribed:

"Christ has no hands but yours."

When I saw that statue with that inscription, I was overwhelmed with emotion.

When Jesus entered a person's circle of suffering, He always ministered to their physical needs, but He also ministered to their spiritual need as well. Ministering to the spiritual needs of man without meeting the physical needs is a heavenly mission with no earthly good. It is not either–or, but both–and. We must feed people's bellies, if we ever hope to feed their souls.

In the story of the Good Samaritan, the robbers put the beaten man in the ditch; the priest and Levite left the man in the ditch; the Samaritan pulled him out of ditch. Jesus never left a person the way he found them. If we leave hurting people the way we found them, how can we call ourselves Christians?

No—Name People

N o doubt, you're familiar with the statement, "It's amazing how much can get done when you don't care who gets the credit." Although we don't always live by the adage, most of us agree with it in principle. The story of the Good Samaritan highlights just such a person—a man who is not even named in the Bible, yet his story has been told as the ultimate example of compassion and altruism for nearly two thousand years. We don't know his name, but God does! But then again, neither do we know the name of the man in the ditch.

Jesus did many of His miracles for "no-name" people. Consider this: We don't know the name of the man who had been crippled for thirty-eight years, lying every day at the pool of Bethesda, until one day, Jesus came along and healed him (John 5:1–15). Nor do we know the name of the woman who touched the hem of His garment and was healed (Mark 5:25–34). We don't know the name of the Samaritan woman at the well, whose life was transformed by her encounter with Christ (John 4:7–42). And we don't know the names of the couple for whom Jesus changed water into wine to keep them from being embarrassed on their wedding day (John 2:1-11). What do all these people have in common? They were all just ordinary people, not "big shots" in politics or in the community. They were no-name people for whom God worked miracles!

God seems to take special pleasure in doing miracles for people that most of us would walk right on by!

Interesting, isn't it, that God seems to take special pleasure in doing miracles for people who most of us would walk right on by. And God uses no-name people to minister to other no-name people. Certainly, God uses celebrities who commit themselves to Him. At Feed The Children, we appreciate our numerous celebrity volunteers who use their positions for more than applause, fame, or money. But for the most part, God delights in using ordinary people like you and me.

The heart is happiest when it beats for others.
ANONYMOUS

The highest exercise of charity is charity toward the uncharitable.
J. S. BUCKMINSTER

In 1989, Mother Teresa visited Phoenix to open a home for the destitute. During that brief visit, she was interviewed by KTAR, one of the largest radio stations in town. In a private moment, the announcer asked Mother Teresa if there was anything he could do for her. He was expecting her to request a contribution or media help to raise money for her new home for the impoverished in Phoenix.

Instead, she replied, "Yes, there is. Find somebody nobody else loves and love them."[iv]

You have not lived today until you have done something for someone who can never repay you.
JOHN BUNYAN

The television cameras weren't running when the Good Samaritan pulled the battered traveler out of the ditch. So often, we are tempted to do our good works so others can see, and if not applaud us, at least be inspired by our example, but the Good Samaritan reminds us that some of our most important deeds will be done when nobody else needs to know. Indeed, Jesus taught that those who do their good deeds to be noticed by the world have received their reward already, but when you do things without fanfare in His name to help hurting people, God notices, and your reward in heaven will be great.

> *Opportunity is missed by most people because it is dressed in overalls, and looks like work.*
> THOMAS EDISON

SOME 1.3 BILLION PEOPLE—ONE THIRD OF THE POPULATION OF THE DEVELOPING WORLD—LIVE ON LESS THAN ONE DOLLAR PER DAY. (UNITED NATIONS DEVELOPMENT PROGRAM)

A Committee of One

T he Good Samaritan was a committee of one. He didn't have a cellular phone to call others for help. He didn't have to consult the professionals before taking action. He didn't have to do a six–month study, or lobby for votes. He saw a need and he took action to meet that need.

We see the "power of one" demonstrated frequently in the Bible. Consider what God did through individuals such as Moses, Joseph, David, and Paul. He can do even greater things through you if you will make yourself available to Him.

The charity that is a trifle to us can be precious to others.
HOMER

I once saw a plaque in a pastor's study that read, "For God so loved the world, He didn't send a committee." How true. While there is strength in numbers and wisdom in a multitude of counselors, trying to satisfy everyone's opinion often stifles more good work for God than it helps. One person really can make a difference, if that person is willing to step out in faith and do what God says to do! The Good Samaritan didn't call a committee meeting; he simply did what he knew that God wanted him to do.

I am only one but I am still one. I cannot do everything, but I can still do something.
And because I cannot do everything, I will not refuse to do the something that I can do.
EDWARD EVERETT HALE

Sometimes when we think about the enormous needs in our world, we become discouraged and feel that one person can't really make a difference. Granted, the needs are staggering, but our God is greater! My dear friend, the late Stan Mooneyham, wisely pointed out that many people are afflicted with "statistical paralysis." They're immobilized by the overwhelming, staggering numbers of people affected by what we call "the hunger problem" or "the poverty problem." Therefore, because they can't help all, they don't help any. But Emily Dickinson's famous poem puts it in perspective for us:

> *If I can stop one heart from breaking,*
> *I shall not live in vain;*
> *If I can ease one life the aching,*
> *Or cool one pain,*
> *Or help one fainting robin*
> *Unto his nest again,*
> *I shall not live in vain.*

Not everybody can do what we do at Feed The Children. But everybody can do something to help relieve hurting people.

One of the greatest aspects of being a committee of one is that you can start just about anywhere, and do almost anything to help those in need, and you don't have to convince anyone to join you.

John Wetteland, the outstanding Major League Baseball pitcher, and the Most Valuable Player of the 1996 World Series, wanted to do something to help feed some children, so for several years, John made a donation to Feed The Children every time his team, the Texas Rangers, won a game. John and his wife, Michelle, also have headed up a toy drive with Ranger fans each year. It started late one night after a game when John and

Michelle saw our television program asking for assistance following a devastating flood. The couple called and said they wanted to help. Since then, we've done toy drives around the country with the help of several Major League Baseball teams.

Michelle's enthusiasm for helping children is infectious, and when the Yankees came to town, Michelle got some of the Yankees' wives involved. Yankees' catcher Joe Girardi and his wife, Kim, got excited about what Michelle was doing, and when Joe was traded to the Chicago Cubs, the toy drive idea went along with the Girardi family and caught on there, as well.

John was just one person who said, "I can make a difference." Funny thing, though, when others see a committee of one operating, they say, "Hey, I can do something like that, too!" and the efforts are multiplied exponentially as more people catch on to what one person can do.

NINETY-SIX PERCENT OF CHRISTIAN FINANCIAL RESOURCES GOES TO SIX PERCENT OF THE WORLD'S POPULATION.

Compassion in Action

"And when he saw him, he had compassion. So he went to him and bandaged his wounds, pouring on oil and wine; and he set him on his own animal, brought him to an inn, and took care of him. On the next day, when he departed, he took out two denarii, gave them to the innkeeper, and said to him, "Take care of him; and whatever more you spend, when I come again, I will repay you.""

LUKE 10:33-35

Imitating the Love of God

One of my former seminary professors, Fred Craddock, tells a story about Burghardt DuBois, a great black educator, sociologist, and historian. Upon completion of studies at Fisk, Harvard, and the University of Berlin, DuBois was convinced that change in the condition of the American black could be affected by careful scientific investigations into truth about black culture in America. As DuBois proceeded, his research was flawless; his graphs and charts impeccable. After waiting several years and hearing not the slightest stir of reform, DuBois had to accept the truth about Truth: just because the truth is available does not mean it will be appropriated.

We see this demonstrated in the story of the Good Samaritan. People know that we should be compassionate toward our

In order to imitate the love of God, we must search for and respond to the needs of the people we come in contact with every day. We cannot simply feel or say love. To be authentic, love must wear work clothes.

CAROLINE MCGEE

neighbor. If I polled one thousand people and asked, "Are you a compassionate person?" about ninety-nine percent would answer, "Yes, I am."

But if I asked, "Is your compassion active or passive?" the majority would have to respond, "Passive."

Knowing that we should be compassionate toward our neighbor and actually being compassionate are two very different things. The priest and the Levite in the story of the Good Samaritan probably were compassionate, but it was the Samaritan who actually did something to meet the need.

The quality of life is determined by its activities.

ARISTOTLE

All It Takes is Love

More than fifteen years ago, my good friend E. V. Hill, pastor of Mount Zion Missionary Baptist church in Los Angeles, was moved to open a food center after he saw hungry people eating out of garbage cans.

"We've got to do something," Pastor Hill said to his wife. "We'll find a building, turn it into a food center, and hire a cook. We'll call it 'The Pastor's Kitchen.' We'll use the extra tithe money the Lord has given us, and we'll feed the hungry people."

Later that night Pastor Hill had a dream. He saw hundreds and hundreds of hungry people standing in a line, waiting to be fed. When Pastor Hill woke up, he knew his vision was more than he could handle alone. This was not to be E. V. Hill's kitchen; feeding hungry people was something that sprang from the heart of God! Pastor Hill decided he'd call the center "The Lord's Kitchen."

About this same time, Pastor Hill's congregation badly needed a new worship center. Seven hundred people attended Sunday school each week in a facility that could hold only half that number. But when Pastor Hill told the congregation about his dream they took the building fund money, bought a facility, and turned it into a center to help feed the poor. Now, years later, thousands of needy families—fathers, mothers, sons, and daughters—eat at The Lord's Kitchen every month.

Pastor Hill and his staff don't charge the needy to eat. Nor are people required to attend Mount Zion church to receive a meal ticket. The church just lets hungry people eat. Yet with no coercion or pressure of any kind, many people come to the Lord each week through The Lord's Kitchen, and they are baptized as new believers. Every Sunday there is a Lord's Kitchen worship service—led by three deacons, two preachers, a music director, and an eighteen-member choir—all people who came to know Jesus through The Lord's Kitchen.

In addition to the kitchen, Pastor Hill's congregation owns a building where people receive free clothing. The church also operates two senior citizens' homes and runs an agency to help high school dropouts find jobs. There's even a dormitory for women and infants who have nowhere else to stay.

A drug rehabilitation program is another way the congregation helps others. Recently, an elderly man, delivered from drug addition, came to the kitchen with his $700 Social Security check and said, "I have a problem."

"What's wrong?" he was asked.

"I don't know what to do with this money," he explained. "Up until now, I'd just turn it over to the drug man and he'd take out what I owed him and give me back $150 or so. This is the first time I don't owe the drug man something. What do I do with all this money?"

"What a wonderful problem to have!" said Pastor Hill. The elderly man was taken to a bank and shown how to open a savings account.

The people of Mount Zion Missionary Baptist Church have put into practice the words of Jesus when He told Peter that if he loved Him, he should "feed my sheep" (John 21:17). And in following this command, the people also have discovered this truth, "He who is kind to the poor lends to the Lord, and He will reward him for what he has done" (Proverbs 19:17, NIV).

And almost as icing on the cake, the congregation discovered that they could never out-give God. Not long ago, they moved into their new worship center. As they had been faithful to reach out and bless others, the blessing was multiplied back to them.

One man. One dream.
One church. One God.
Thousands helped. Thousands fed.
Thousands loved. Thousands saved.

I want nothing to do with any religion concerned with keeping the masses satisfied to live in hunger, filth, and ignorance.

EDGAR SNOW

To allow the hungry man to remain hungry
would be blasphemy against God and one's neighbor,
for what is nearest to God is precisely the need of one's neighbor.
It is for the love of Christ, which belongs as much to the
hungry man as to myself, that I share my bread with him
and that I share my dwelling with the homeless.
If the hungry man does not attain to faith,
then the fault falls on those who refused him bread.
To provide the hungry man with bread
is to prepare the way for the coming of grace.

DIETRICH BONHOEFFER

Help Along the Way

A wonderful by-product comes to those who help hurting people—you will be blessed with great friendships along the way as people work with you. No doubt, the Good Samaritan made a friend of the innkeeper who housed the man beaten by the robbers. The innkeeper was probably impressed with the Samaritan's compassion and integrity, and he might have felt just a little better about himself for being involved in an effort to help another human being.

Over the years, I've been privileged to forge many strong friendships with people who have been looking for ways to do the works of God. And God has taught me some lessons along the way, as well. For instance, when I was thirty-eight years of age, and already involved in a relief effort, I finally discovered who my "neighbor" really is.

In 1986, I took a television crew with me to Africa to do some filming for an upcoming program. Early one morning, we were driving down a dusty road in the Rift Valley, one of the most impoverished places on earth, when we came upon a group of about twenty-five women, each one carrying four to six five-gallon cans on her head. We pulled over and asked, "What's going on?"

"We're in the midst of a terrible drought," one of the women replied. "We're hoping that two of us can get on the next bus that comes along. We'll put all the women's water cans on top of the bus, then we'll go into Nairobi and fill up the cans. It will take us most of the day to fill up the cans. In the evening, we'll load the water on a bus and come back where the other women can meet us, and carry the water to our village. We don't have any water in our village, so we must do this twice a week."

"What a great story this would make," I thought. I asked the women if they minded if I did some filming. They didn't.

We started rolling film just about the time the next bus rolled down the road. The dusty vehicle lumbered to a stop, and the driver stepped off. "Sorry," he said, "but the bus is full. I can't take any of you to town, or any of your cans."

The women just stood there, dejection written across their faces. They were devastated. They had to get water! How were they going to survive?

Suddenly Dave Smith, my cameraman, rushed over to me and said, "Larry, the camera just stopped. But don't worry. It's brand new and I should have it fixed quickly." He sat down under a tree and began working on the camera.

The bus took off, leaving behind a swirl of dust—and thirty anxious, thirsty women.

About an hour later, my cameraman came over and said, "Larry, I'm sorry. There's something drastically wrong with this camera. It just won't run."

"I don't believe this," I muttered. "Here I am, with a crew of seven people, and we've come half way around the world from the United States to shoot a television program, and our stupid camera won't work!"

Then the Lord hit me right between my jaded eyes. WHAM!

"You know, Larry," He said, "these women have a much greater need than you do. They don't have any water. That's life–threatening. You don't have any footage. That's inconvenient."

God and I had a good talk about priorities in that dust bowl. Well, actually, He talked and I listened. The result was that my camera crew and I sent a man to town to help the women. He found and paid for a water truck, and the driver took an entire load of water to the women's village, allowing each of them to fill their pots for a week or more. Mission of mercy accomplished. And not a bit of it on film.

When I returned to the United States, I re-read the Bible, every single word of it, with a new perspective and an illuminated mind regarding what the Bible says we are to do for the poor. "Obviously, I've missed an important point," I thought, and I had! As I studied the Scripture, God impressed on my heart that from the beginning of His book to the end, He wants His people—Larry Jones included, you included—to take care of the widow, the fatherless, the orphan, the hungry, the poor, and the oppressed. Those are His priorities; they ought to be mine.

A few days later I got a telephone call from the Oak Ridge Boys, a country music group also known for its gospel roots. "We're doing a concert in Nice, France, and want to donate the proceeds to you, no strings attached," they informed me.

I thought for a moment, knowing the money could be used to feed hungry children, but instead I said, "I'll tell you what I'd like to do. I'd like to go to Africa and dig four water wells, each costing $25,000-$40,000 depending on how deeply we must dig. I'll use your donation as seed money, raise the rest, and then I'll name each one of those four wells after one of you guys."

The Oak Ridge Boys loved the idea, and today a well provides fresh water to those women's village, plus three other villages. All because God let me see His priorities and provided help from some friends.

Who knows what God might do through you and your friends, when you start seeing life's interruptions as God's opportunities?

When Pope Paul VI was a Cardinal Archbishop, a social worker came to him saying that he was without means to feed the hungry.
"My furniture is at your disposal. Sell some to feed the needy," replied the Cardinal.

He's Not Busted Anymore

You might have heard the low, gravelly voice of John Conlee, the country singer perhaps best known for his remake of the Ray Charles hit *I'm Busted*. The song goes something like this: "The bills are not paid and the kids are not fed, and I'm busted. The rent's comin' due and my baby needs shoes, and I'm busted."

One night when John sang that song, people got out of their seats, walked to the stage, and laid a few dollar bills down by John's feet—jokingly, I imagine, so John wouldn't be busted. Before the night was over, John had collected $58.

A few days later, John called me and said, "I'm going to send you $58. Please use it to buy fuel for your trucks to feed hungry children in Appalachia."

And I said, "Sure," and thought nothing more about it.

A few weeks later, a friend sent me a clipping from the *Chicago Tribune*, stating that every time John Conlee sings *Busted*, people come up to the stage and lay down dollar bills.

One Saturday night, my mother called and asked, "Are you by any chance watching the Grand Ole' Opry?"

"No, Mom, I'm not."

"Well, you better turn it on. I've never seen anything like it. People are lined up in the aisles, and this guy's down there singing, and everybody's givin' him a dollar for Feed The Children."

Shortly after that, I received another call from John Conlee. "Larry, would you come down to Nashville and appear on television with me?" John asked. "Because now I've got almost $10,000."

Some time later, John called again. "I'm up to $100,000."

And before long, John Conlee presented Feed The Children with a check for $150,000! John said, "Don't thank me; it's been my fans donating the money." If John ever was, he wasn't busted anymore. That's what can happen when somebody gets the urge to give of himself.

Another singer called me one day and said, "I'm going to do a Christmas album, and I'd like you to come along with me as I promote it."

I agreed to go with him, and a few days later we took off. At the first press conference, a reporter asked the recording artist, "How much are you going to give Feed The Children?

Garth Brooks replied, "One dollar off each album." That was the beginning of a longstanding relationship between one of the music industry's most successful performers and hungry, hurting families. For the next eight years, a Feed The Children tractor–trailer truck followed Garth Brooks on tour around the country. In every city where Garth performed, thousands of pounds of food were collected at his concerts and distributed to needy families.

God will give His blessings to you, if He can get them through you!

Remember how it started? I gave a little Haitian boy twenty cents, and God has multiplied that little bit into more than $78 million in cash, which helped us to move more than $383 million in food, medicine, and educational materials. [i]

The Bible says "He who has pity on the poor lends to the Lord, And He will pay back what he has given" (Proverbs 19:17). I've discovered that the Lord pays back at an enormous interest rate! When God leads you to help a hurting person, He will make a way for you to do it. You just need to be an available conduit through which He can pour His resources. God will give His blessings to you, if He can get them through you!

We Are the Safety Net

A few years ago, I testified before a congressional committee on welfare reform. I told them, "I agree, welfare needs to be reformed, but when it is, you need to provide a safety net so no child falls through the cracks."

The chairman of the committee looked back at me and said, "Mr. Jones, you are the safety net."

Charities, churches, synagogues, and food pantries have been given the responsibility to provide the basic needs for the millions of Americans who suffer from nothing more than being poor. Sure, there will be people who take advantage—always have been, always will be—but these numbers are small when compared to the overwhelming majority of hurting people who simply need help.

Consider Appalachia, one of God's most beautiful landscapes, nestled in the rolling hills of Kentucky, but also an area of our country where the poverty rate is extremely high. Generations of people in Appalachia have earned their living working in the coal mines. Now, the mining industry has dwindled to the point that in one county, for every single mining job that becomes available, fifty men apply for that position.

My wife and I visited Appalachia with singer Ricky Skaggs, who grew up in eastern Kentucky. Taking with us food and medical supplies, we planned to help where the need was greatest. Unfortunately, the need was great everywhere.

The first family we visited lived in a shack that the grandfather had built out of scraps. Electrical wiring dangled from the ceiling. The walls were rotting on the outside, eroding on the inside. Every drop of water the family used came from a well at the end of a dirt road, right next to a busy highway. The lid to the well was crumbling and ill fitting, allowing in all sorts of dirt, bugs, vermin, and debris. The water was unsanitary, but it was all the family had.

When six-year-old Sally* and seven-year-old Tommy* got up in the morning, they didn't run down the hall to the bathroom. Instead, they climbed a narrow path to the outhouse. Because there was no bathtub, cleaning up meant standing up in a basin on the porch. But to the children, having a bath was a way of maintaining some dignity. And for these two little kids dignity was about as hard to come by as a clean dress or a new pair of jeans.

Ricky Skaggs asked Sally and Tommy if they had eaten that day, and the children indicated that they had not had a single bite. Ricky was outraged. "You know," he told me, "when a child hasn't eaten by late afternoon, chances are pretty good that child isn't going to eat all day. Yet, I know these people don't want handouts. They don't want to live this way. They need some hope. They need a future."

I explained to Ricky that families in Appalachia, as in many other regions across America, have to answer tough questions every month. "Do we eat or have heat? Do we buy shoes or do we buy food? Do we get a tire for the car so we can go to work, or do we get medicine for the kids so they can go to school?"

Frances, Ricky, and I visited another family later that day. Only the names of the children were different. The same stark reality, the same bleak conditions, the same blank stares from tear-filled eyes, far too old for such little souls, seared into our hearts.

Eight-year-old Bobbie* and six-year-old Billie* lived with their mother in another of those shacks. They had no indoor plumbing, no fresh running water. Twila*, the boys' mother, hauled eighteen to twenty buckets of water per day from a dirty well. "It's hard," Twila told us, "real hard. But most of all, it's hard to listen to the taunting

*Names have been changed to respect these people's identities.

from other people about where we live. My boys understood all too well that they probably won't ever have nuthin' more. It's a process of barely gettin' by and makin' do with what we got."

Frances, Ricky, and I spent some time talking with the youngsters. They showed us their toys: a dump truck minus two wheels, a basketball that wouldn't hold air, and a cast-away-by-the-side-of-the-road bike that rolled on the rims of flat tires.

When the boys smiled, they showed us their teeth, apparently something else they were learning to live without. Billie pointed to all the places in his mouth that caused him pain. "This one hurts and this one. . . ." Billie's teeth were literally falling out from lack of good nutrition.

"I had no idea," Ricky said, "that people in eastern Kentucky were living like this. You expect it in Third World countries, but to see it right here in my own backyard, right here in America, it's just unbelievable. I can get in my truck and I can drive back home, but I'll never be the same."

Frances, Ricky, and I walked away in silence after giving what we could to that needy family. That day, they had food, and the next day, and maybe on into the next week. But what then? There's not a safety net big enough to catch them, or the many others like them. As much as we try, and as much as we do, and as much as friends like Ricky Skaggs help, there are simply too many children who fall through the cracks.

Our politicians have a penchant for closing their speeches with the phrase, "God bless America!" God bless America? He already has! God shake America to wake up and see the human need all around us!

Do the little things that nobody sees.
LARRY JONES

True Star Power

I n the small hours of the morning, motion picture star Melanie Griffith was feeding her baby while her husband, Antonio Banderas, was asleep. She turned on the television and what she saw affected her deeply—it was one of Feed The Children's television programs regarding the plight of hungry children in America. Not wanting to disturb her husband, she reached for her lipstick pencil and used it to write the Feed The Children phone number on a mirror.

The next day, Melanie picked up the phone in California and called our offices in Oklahoma City. "Larry Jones," she said, "I want to do something to help. No child in the United States should have to struggle with the burden those little kids carry."

I had not had the privilege of meeting Melanie before that time. My only awareness of her was as a star of the big screen. I was soon to discover that Melanie is a star in another right, as well. After conversations between my staff and hers, Melanie arranged to accompany me on a four-day tour of some of the problem areas in America where the poverty statistics are high. Throughout the United States, one in four children struggles with hunger, and in the more remote parts of our country, the statistics are much worse. We had no trouble finding places for Melanie to visit.

It was a dreary, damp morning when we arrived in one town. We made our way down a road to a dented and rusty trailer. The landlord had divided the trailer in half, and two single moms and six children lived there, cramped sardine–style into two tiny rooms. Eight people shared a single bedroom, a room equipped with nothing more than mattresses on the floor, no pillows, no sheets. Holes in the walls allowed cold wind to blow in; holes in the ceiling allowed a similar intrusion of cold rain. The rent for this housing was one hundred dollars a week. This was not in a Third World country; this was in a town in the United States of America, the most affluent nation in the history of the world!

Both mothers worked at minimum wage jobs, one at night, the other during the day to avoid childcare expenses. Neither made enough money to adequately feed their children. Both, however, made "too much" money to qualify for a government food stamp program. They were caught up in the game known as the "working poor," a game they faithfully played by the rules but had no chance of winning.

Around the corner, Melanie and I met another single mom with three children. Their electricity and water had been turned off. Not able to make it through a month before their money ran out, no matter how well income and expenses were juggled, they were on the verge of eviction. Options exhausted, the only thing these four had in abundance was depression.

I remarked to Melanie, "Every single day of the year, conditions like these exist. Twelve million children right here in the United States, in the land of the free and the home of the brave, suffer the pain of gnawing hunger. Add to that the millions of children without a home, living in shelters, cars, or in the streets, and you can see why I say on our television programs that America is in the throes of a national tragedy."

Shaken by what she saw, Melanie shook her head and fought back the tears. "I'm amazed," she said, "that in a country with so much wealth, we can't take better care of our own people."

In Nashville, two Feed The Children semi-trucks unloaded food and supplies for the area's hungry. Then we went on to Harlem, where over 2,200 families lined up to get a box of food and health items. We stopped in Dallas at Planet Hollywood, a restaurant chain in which Melanie owned an interest. Four FTC trucks unloaded food for relief agencies there. The last stop was to San Diego, where we distributed food to several local charities. In all, more than 334,000 pounds of food was delivered to thousands of needy families during that trip.

Melanie was so moved that she encouraged Planet Hollywood restaurants across the United States to help feed our country's hungry children. If you visit one of those restaurants, you'll see movie and television memorabilia. But if you're lucky, you might also get a glimpse of a woman with real star power, a person who refused to sit by and do nothing when her neighbors needed help.

IN ONE STUDY, CHILDREN WHO WERE SEVERELY UNDERWEIGHT WERE FOUND TO BE TWO TO EIGHT TIMES MORE LIKELY TO DIE WITHIN THE FOLLOWING YEAR AS CHILDREN OF NORMAL WEIGHT FOR THEIR AGE.
(UNICEF)

How Can I Keep Balance?

With such horrendous human need in our world, many people wonder how we can even sleep at night: there's always another mouth to be fed, another person who needs medical attention, another need somewhere. But God doesn't expect us to live in constant frustration. He wants us to enjoy life. He doesn't want you to fret with guilt every time you eat a good meal. God does expect us to be bridges over which His blessings can flow to others.

The late Stan Mooneyham worked alongside of me for five years after he left World Vision, another organization that helps hurting people. Stan confided to Mother Teresa one day in Calcutta. He shared with her the discomfort of feeling like a yo-yo. He was helping hungry and homeless people one day, and then the next day he was back in his comfortable, affluent world. He said, partially in jest, "I think I should be more comfortable if I took the vow of poverty and came here to join you." Mother Teresa replied, "You must allow God to make you a bridge without asking you."

Most of us want to tell God how we are going to do great things for Him, but that's not how it works. The key is to be faithful in doing the little things, the things that nobody sees. Leave the rest up to God.

I shall pass through this world but once. Any good thing, therefore, that I can do, or any kindness that I can show to any human being, let me do it now. Let me not defer it or neglect it, for I shall not pass this way again.
STEPHEN GRELET, NINETEENTH CENTURY AUTHOR

International 911

I magine that you hear a phone ringing in your home. You hurry to check your caller I.D. to see who is calling before you answer. You don't recognize the number, so you decide not to answer the call. Again and again, the phone rings, but you choose to ignore it. You change the channel on the television set, or turn the music up louder. Anything . . . just don't answer the call!

Later, you learn that the person who had been calling you was actually trying to place a 911 emergency call, but had somehow dialed your number instead. How do you think you might feel? How would you feel if you were the person making the call?

The fact is the phone is ringing . . . and ringing . . . and ringing! Desperate, hurting people are calling for help, but nobody is answering the call. Instead, we turn up the volume on our distractions.

In 1984-85, the tragic Ethiopian famine received worldwide attention thanks to Bob Geldoff's highly publicized "Band-Aid" concert and the hit song "We are the World." Despite such efforts to raise awareness and support, approximately one million people perished, largely due to the delay in international response. Such pandemic death needn't happen again, but sadly, many African countries are once again on the sun-caked cusp of a famine that threatens to surpass the disaster of the mid-eighties. Meanwhile, distractions continue to keep well-fed countries from giving even meager supplies of food and water to people traveling days in search of help. The long-distance "prize" goes to a woman who walked 135 miles in hopes of finding food for her family members, five of whom—including the father—died along the way.

Granted, war is a major factor in causing famine, along with drought weather conditions. But should politics steer our pity away from hearing the 911 call and from helping to relieve a potentially massive international disaster?

When a legal expert asked Jesus to define "neighbor," Jesus answered with the story of the Good Samaritan. The Samaritan didn't parse words or let cultural bias color his conscience. He took the Jewish man who had been left to die to an inn and paid for everything he needed to heal. Jesus told His questioner to go and do likewise. Why would He demand less of us? The Russian writer Leo Tolstoy said, "My bread belongs to me only when I know that no one starves while I eat."

Today, we have the privilege of being a neighbor and our brothers' keeper. In the first book of the Bible, God asked Cain where his brother Abel was. Cain retorted, "Am I my brother's keeper?" In the New Testament, the question posed by the lawyer in the story of the Good Samaritan was, "Who is my neighbor?" Two thousand years later, we're still asking the same question! Something is wrong with us. Why haven't we discovered the answer?

Recently, the Horn of Africa was on the brink of large-scale deprivation and suffering. Some experts predicted twelve million people could be affected, and we can prevent thousands, maybe millions, from protracted hunger, sickness, and death. From a region too poor, weak, and war–ravaged to pick up the telephone, we are once again hearing the 911 call, the desperate cry into the mouthpiece.

The international 911 is ringing—will you please answer the call?

LARRY JONES

Many of the voices on the other end of the 911 calls belong to innocent children. In Africa right now, experts estimate they will need 80,000 orphanages, housing five hundred children in each, simply to take care of the children whose parents have died or will die soon of AIDS. Those babies did nothing immoral. They did not choose a life of drug addiction, or other deadly lifestyles. Some of them were born HIV–positive. Others are suffering because of the sins of their parents, and multitudes are bereft of their families because of the AIDS epidemic.

In Uganda, many Christian families are attempting to place the children in extended families, but the problem of feeding all those children is going to be massive.

An international 911 call is ringing for every person. How will you respond? Remember, the job is too big for any one of us, but not too big for all of us!

TODAY, ABOUT ONE IN FIVE NEWBORNS IN THE DEVELOPING WORLD WEIGHS TOO LITTLE, LESS THAN 2.5 KG. (5.5 LBS.), AND THE GROWTH OF NEARLY FOUR IN EVERY TEN CHILDREN IS STUNTED.
(UNICEF)

War Babies

At Feed The Children we've been caring for hungry children for more than two decades. We've seen horrendous suffering in our work, but nowhere has the devastation to children been worse, or more needlessly tragic, than during times of war.

In the past ten years, twelve million children have been left homeless, and another one million orphaned, because of war in countries such as Bosnia, Angola, Somalia, El Salvador, Kosovo, Uganda, and Afghanistan. Five million children have been maimed, many after crawling as scouts across fields teeming with landmines ahead of the "troops" composed of ten–, twelve–, and fifteen–year–old children conscripted into service. Add to these victims the thousands of children who witnessed executions of family members or who even were forced to kill their own loved ones. It's hard for most of us to comprehend the heartache caused to children in the ravages of war.

And then there are the brave little warriors who survive months and years of fighting, only to find that life after war is filled with miseries of poverty, hunger, and fear.

Are the lives of these children, each one fashioned by the hand of God, really worth so little? Our unconcern, all too often, answers that question as "yes."

On the other hand, miracles can happen when you, as a committee of one, dare to get involved in meeting human needs. Often your committee of one is expanded as others see the need, as well. That's what happened in the life of one young woman.

Marija (Maria) Topalovic, one of nine children, grew up in a home filled with laughter and love. As a youngster in the late 1980's, her life was typical of most girls: days filled with school, evenings filled with play, experiments with makeup, and dreams of dancing with a handsome boy.

But that was before the war in Bosnia, before Marija's world was shattered, before her neighbors—Muslim, Croatian, and Serb—began to distrust one another. Then in December 1993, Marija's childhood was abruptly changed again, in a way that would last forever.

Marija, her brother, and her father had returned that quiet afternoon to poke around the rubble of what had been their home in central Bosnia. Still standing, but badly damaged by mortar fire, the burned-out walls of the house now stood as a ghostly reminder of happier times. The Topalovics planned to retrieve some desperately needed canned food stored in the basement. Marija's brother lagged behind while the daughter and father approached their home. But before they could begin their task, another round of mortar fire began without warning.

Amid the scream and roar of this rain of terror, Marija and her father ran toward an underground bunker. An explosion ricocheted off the hills and a shell whistled out of the sky, landing directly between the two of them. Marija was catapulted into the air and slammed back to the ground. "Daddy! Help me, Daddy!" Marija cried. There was no answer.

Marija's brother saw what had happened and ran back to his fallen father. He cradled his father's head in his arms. "I love you," the father said, then died.

Marija's brother then ran to her. When Marija tried to stand, she couldn't move. "I can't get up!" she cried. Looking down at the blood flowing on the ground all around her, the brother said, "Honey, you don't have any legs."

Marija's brother carried her mangled body to a nearby church, which had been used as a makeshift hospital. There, by candlelight, without running water, heat, or much medication for pain, the doctors amputated the shattered ruins of Marija's legs above her knees.

Mortar shells still flew the day Frances and I arrived in Marija's town in Bosnia. We spent the night in a house without electricity or heat, but blazing, incoming mortars lit the sky all night long. Feed The Children had been involved in sending relief supplies to Bosnia for some time, and we had arrived in that country to view our efforts firsthand and to tape some segments for our television program. During our stay, we visited the church that had become the hospital.

The sanctuary was filled, not with wounded soldiers, but with children. Bed after bed held the broken body of an innocent victim: Allen had taken a shell in his stomach. Boyan was blinded by shrapnel. Angelina had been shot by a sniper, and the bullet lodged near her heart couldn't be removed in such difficult conditions. The pain and suffering were overwhelming.

Then we came upon Marija, a pretty fourteen-year-old with dark eyes and dark hair. We visited for a moment and then the nurse pulled back Marija's blanket. I was appalled and amazed at her condition. Here was a young girl, alone, afraid, and forgotten, whose hopes had been destroyed. Yet, here also was a young girl who possessed a strong resolve to live.

"Marija," I said through an interpreter, "I can't make any promises, but I'll see what we can do. I believe that someday, someone will help you walk again."

Later that week, I returned to the United States, but one morning I heard on the news that children were being airlifted by helicopter out of Bosnia. I paused long enough to watch the report on television, and suddenly I saw Marija being lifted into the helicopter. I could hardly believe my eyes!

When I got to the office, I set about getting her brought to the United States. Don Richardson of Feed The Children traced Marija to a hospital in Italy. He arranged for her to be transferred to Zurich, and from there American Airlines provided free transportation for Marija, her mother, and her three sisters to New York. The Saint Maritz hotel put them up for free, and the next day, Marija and I appeared as guests on the ABC-TV program *Good Morning America*. I introduced Marija and her plight, and almost immediately the phones in our offices started ringing.

A team of doctors at Baptist Hospital in Oklahoma City offered their services to care for Marija. A good friend of mine donated a condo. A furniture dealer provided furnishings. A discount club chipped in housewares. A rental car agency offered unlimited transportation. A domino effect—one miracle leading to another— was set into motion as people recognized the need and volunteered their help—all for free! The committee of one often turns into an army of people volunteering to help.

It's important that you do what God leads you to do at the moment, because that gets the ball rolling. If you miss the opportunity, or if you refuse to participate in God's plan, you stop not just one miracle from happening. You might stop a multitude of miracles.

One of the most exciting offers of help for Marija came from one of the country's foremost prosthetics specialists, Scott Sabolich, who "just happened" to reside in Oklahoma City. He offered to customize and fit Marija with a new set of legs—at no charge.

I have never seen so many different circumstances come together so quickly. It was a miracle that Marija had survived the mortar blast, and the miracles kept on coming.

Hope that had died in Bosnia was sparked back to life. And thus began the long journey for Marija—a journey that would take her out of harm's way to a new country, a new family, and a new future. Today, Marija Topalovic is a beautiful young woman whom Frances and I have grown to love and respect. She's determined to live life to the fullest. She walks proudly on prosthetic legs. She speaks fluent English. She drives a car that can be operated using only her hands, with controls similar to a motorcycle for acceleration and braking. Choosing to stay in Oklahoma City, she graduated from high school, and is working toward her college degree.

"And then what?" I asked Marija recently.

"I want to do something for the children—for the children left behind in Bosnia. If there was hope for me, there's hope for them. I want to see God's love spread from heart to heart."

When I first looked into Marija's eyes those many years ago, I knew she was someone special. Now I know why.

Rabbi Edward Paul Cohen tells this story:
A German widow hid Jewish refugees in her home during World War II. When her best friends learned of her illegal activities, they were alarmed and extremely fearful for her safety.
"You're risking your life!" they warned her.
"I know that," she replied.
"Then why do you persist in this foolishness?"
"I am doing it because the time is now and I am here."

The time is now for you and me, if we will only allow God to interrupt us long enough to see the opportunities before us.

Go and Do Likewise

Then Jesus said to him, "Go and do likewise."

LUKE 10:37

Let's Get to Work

At the conclusion of His story about the Good Samaritan, Jesus asked the Jewish lawyer which of the three men had proved to be a neighbor to the man who had been beaten and robbed. The answer must have caught in the lawyer's throat. Much to his dismay, he had to admit that it had been the Samaritan—the outcast, the hated, despised fellow—who acted more righteously than the Jewish priest or the Levite.

Jesus, however, cut to the heart of the matter. Regardless of race or religion, He said, "Go and do likewise" (Luke 10:37). That is still His command to us today. One of God's biggest problems, however, is absenteeism in the field. The people He has called are not answering, and even many of those who have answered the call, aren't showing up for work.

One of God's biggest problems is absenteeism in the field.

It is not enough merely to exist. It's not enough to say,
"I'm earning enough to support my family.
I do my work well. I'm a good father, husband, churchgoer."
That's all very well, but you must do something more.
Seek always to do some good, somewhere.
Every man has to seek in his own way to realize his true worth.
You must give some time to your fellow man.
Even if it's a little thing, do something for those who need help,
something for which you get no pay but the privilege of doing it.
For remember, you don't live in a world all your own.
Your brothers are here, too.

ALBERT SCHWEITZER

That Oh, So Inadequate Feeling

M ost of us feel inadequate at times, much like Moses when God spoke to him from the burning bush and told him that he was the man to lead the Hebrew people out of slavery into the Promised Land. Moses immediately thought of his own inadequacies and began making excuses to God for why he couldn't do what God had just commanded him to do. But God is not swayed by our excuses. He does not require us to be tremendously talented or super intelligent. All He asks is that we make ourselves available to Him.

When Frances and I began doing the work that eventually evolved into Feed The Children, we often asked, "Lord, why have you chosen us to do this? We don't have a clue about what we're doing!" We had no mentors or previous experience in securing and delivering food to people. We had no idea how to raise the necessary money to finance such an operation. All we knew was that the need was great, and we were available to God. After a while, we realized that part of the reason God chose us was because we didn't know how to run such an enormous operation in our own power. Because we didn't know what we were doing, we were totally dependent on God to get it done. We had no excuses.

You might convince your spouse, or your children, or your pastor that you don't know what to do to help hurting people; you might even convince yourself, but you'll never convince God of that. As Theodore Roosevelt once said, "In any moment of decision, the best thing you can do is the right thing, the next best thing is the wrong thing, and the worst thing you can do is nothing."

Benjamin Franklin used to ask himself when he got up every morning, "What good can I do today?" At the end of the day, he asked himself again, "What good have I done today?" We need to ask ourselves those same questions, especially in light of Jesus' command to "Go and do likewise." If we don't, we will often discover that we've lived the day totally for ourselves. While some people may applaud living each day for yourself, God will not give you a standing ovation for such selfish living.

God will not give you a standing ovation for selfish living.

Help one person. Just one. How many people did the Samaritan help? One. Yet his example has stirred people to action throughout history. The Samaritan wasn't concerned about leaving a legacy; he simply met the need he saw. Mother Teresa often pointed out that Jesus didn't say, "Love the whole world." He said, "Love one another."

When Mother Teresa was asked how you feed a billion starving people, her answer was, "One at a time."

Make yourself necessary to somebody.
RALPH WALDO EMERSON

Powerful Words from a Little Lady

If you don't get satisfaction from doing something on a small scale,
you won't get any more satisfaction doing it on a global scale.
Nothing, multiplied by five billion, is still nothing.

We feel that what we are doing is just a drop in the ocean,
but the ocean would be less because of that missing drop.

We do no great things, only small things with great love.

Love is a fruit in season at all times, and within reach of every hand.

MOTHER TERESA

Avoiding Compassion Burnout

I'm frequently asked by the media, "Why did you choose to bring food to this particular city today?"

"We have a room with a large map of the United States on the wall," I tell them. "We go into the room, turn out the lights. We throw a dart at the map, and then turn the lights back on. Wherever the dart sticks, that's where we go."

Usually the members of the media laugh.

Then I say, "It doesn't matter where the dart hits. There are hungry children in that town. There's a need there."

The job of meeting needs is bigger than Feed The Children. We need help and everyone has something to offer. For instance, once when we were conducting a food drop, a man drove up in a BMW and asked for two boxes of food. He wanted to take them to some needy families that he knew. Of course, we gave him the food. It doesn't matter whose name is on the delivery, as long as people are helped!

We need help and everyone has something to offer.

LARRY JONES

During a Feed The Children food drop in Port Gibson, Mississippi, a seventy–year–old woman, walking with a cane, came through the food lines. We loaded her up with a box of food weighing twenty-six pounds, and a seventeen–pound turkey, as well. She was so grateful for the food that she nearly wept on the street. But now she had another problem. She asked one of our volunteer workers, "Will you help me carry this food over to the bus stop?"

The volunteer gladly assisted the woman, but as I watched her go, I couldn't help but wonder, "Who will help the woman when she gets home . . ."

We really don't understand the problems of the poor.

On the other hand, I don't allow myself to be overcome with concern about what I can't do. If I am doing what I can do, then I can sleep at night. I'm reminded that Jesus didn't heal or feed all the hurting and hungry children in Israel during His life on earth . . . but He helped and fed some. He lived life to the fullest, attended wedding receptions, as well as religious festivals, and took time to rest. Most importantly, He renewed His spiritual strength in prayer. With Jesus as my example, I refuse to allow the enormous need or the logistical nightmares of transporting millions of pounds of food to overwhelm me. I simply try to help as best I can whenever the Lord places a need in the scope of my awareness. I take the first step of obedience and trust Him for the next.

HALF OF SOUTH ASIA'S CHILDREN ARE MALNOURISHED.
IN AFRICA, ONE OF EVERY THREE CHILDREN IS UNDERWEIGHT,
AND IN SEVERAL COUNTRIES OF THE CONTINENT,
THE NUTRITIONAL STATUS OF CHILDREN IS WORSENING.
(UNICEF)

People Versus Things

N early 35,000 children under five years of age die each day in developing countries, mainly from malnutrition and other poverty–related, preventable diseases [i]. The terrible numbers have pummeled us for so long that we are no longer shocked. We let the statistics roll off as we continue our personal quests for success or material things. Most people in the United States still live by the adage, "The one who dies with the most toys wins." We forget, of course, that the one who dies with the most toys still dies.

You can't have everything . . . where would you put it?
STEPHEN WRIGHT

When a group of international leaders first came to the United States a few years ago, they were given tours of great American cities, such as our space program's mission control facilities. As they prepared to board their plane back home, a reporter asked, "What impressed you most about America?"

"The size of your garbage cans," was the reply.

Americans waste ninety-six billion pounds of food every year! We literally throw away twenty-five percent of our nation's food supply. We have become a "throwaway society," and we still have far too much left over. Have you ever noticed the enormous amount of surplus items we have? Any weekend, the local newspapers are filled with notices of garage sales and "flea markets." Why? Because we have become addicted to credit cards, buying things we don't need, with money we

We buy things we don't need, with money we don't have, to impress people we don't like.

don't have, to impress people we don't like. Then we end up selling what we bought for ten cents on the dollar at a garage sale, or giving it to charity and thinking we've accomplished something.

Fourteen days before President John F. Kennedy died, he addressed the Protestant Council of New York and urged church leaders to support foreign aid. He deplored the fact that assistance from the United States had dropped to a mere four percent of the national budget. President Kennedy said, "Surely the Americans of the 1960s can do half as well as the Americans of the 1950s. Surely we are not going to throw away our hopes and means for peaceful progress in an outburst of imitation and frustration. I do not want it said of us what T. S. Eliot said of others some years ago: 'These were a decent people; their only monument: the asphalt road and a thousand lost golf balls.' I think we can do better than that."

Even in the church, we are prone to think bigger is better, that more matters more. Our churches have followed middle-class America in our quest for affluence. Certainly, we want to build beautiful, functional churches, but what good is a magnificent sanctuary if Jesus is sleeping out on the sidewalk? Christians are to be salt and light in the world. But salt only preserves what it touches. And even a single, tiny light brings hope to those who are in darkness.

Salt only preserves what it touches.

It's difficult for overfed, comfortably dressed, and luxuriously housed people to hear God's call to the poor.

The full belly doesn't believe in hunger.

It's Not Easy, But It's Worth It

I t always costs something to care for hurting people. Don't ever get the idea that compassion and caring are free and easy; they aren't. They can rip your insides out sometimes, wrenching every ounce of energy and emotion you can muster. But if God favors your efforts, it is worth it.

When people ask me, "What is the secret to Feed The Children's success?" I can only answer that we continue to pray for favor with God and mankind. But that doesn't mean we don't have problems, or suffer disappointments, failures, mistakes, or sin.

Remember where Joseph was when God favored him? He was in prison! It's often in the pits, prisons, and other pressure points in life that we can find God's opportunities if we look carefully.

The Apostle Paul endured beatings, shipwreck, imprisonment, and other hardships as a result of his efforts to spread God's message of love and reconciliation. Besides the abuse he received from his detractors, he also carried about a "thorn in the flesh" for which he prayed three times for God to remove. But God didn't. Paul accepted the thorn as part of the price to do what he knew God wanted him to do.

Throughout the Bible, and down through history, you will find individuals who were greatly used by God to touch the world, but they were not immune to life's difficulties, discouragement, or the effects of other people's sinful actions. Nor are we.

For instance, on one occasion, a ship on which we had contracted cargo space sank to the bottom of the sea carrying an entire load of food, food in containers that we were sending to hungry families.

Selfishness and greed often rear their ugly heads in opposition to compassion. In another country, the authorities attempted to hold a load of wheat in their warehouses and overcharge us fees for unloading the ship. Our representative negotiated down the "bill" only to discover that the wheat had disappeared. When a man finally agreed to help us retrieve the missing wheat, he was murdered in the parking lot.

At that point, I appealed personally to the president of the country. Two men eventually were prosecuted and sent to prison for theft, and our insurance paid us for what was stolen. The murderer was never found, although the government assumed that the thieves were somehow connected to the man's death.

Often the work of helping hurting people will crush your own heart. On one occasion, we took a film crew and arranged for some food to be sent to the northernmost part of Kosovo. When we first arrived at the United Nations checkpoint only a few people were there, but soon we saw long lines of refugees stumbling toward the boarder. Many of them had walked for days with no food or water. People were collapsing on the ground. Most of them had experienced horrendous abuse at the hands of their oppressors. For instance, one woman told me how the soldiers made her and her two daughters leave, and when they had gone out the door, they heard two shots as her sons were killed.

During a famine in Ethiopia, I had a plane packed with food in Kenya, and we wanted to deliver it to the starving people. But the government of Ethiopia would not grant us permission to land. I prayed for three days to no avail, crying out, "Why, God? Why?" We never did get that particular load of food into the country, and I still don't understand why, but one day, I will. For now my job is simply to be faithful in what God has instructed me to do.

At times such as those, if I were not convinced that the work is

God's and not mine, my heart would not be able to stand another day of the human suffering we have seen. Much of the world's pain rises from man's inhumanity to his fellow man and the selfishness of sinful men and women, but I believe that God can change human hearts, so we offer food, water, clothing, and whatever aid we can in His name. We often rely on Romans 8:28—"And we know that all things work together for good to those who love God, to those who are the called according to His purpose."

Helping people is not without risk, danger, or frustration. Everything does not always turn out rosy. Similar to the characters in Charles Sheldon's classic book *In His Steps*, sometimes we do what Jesus would do and everything works out wonderfully; at other times people do what God wants them to do, and it seems as though the bottom falls out. When Pastor E. V. Hill and his congregation opened The Lord's Kitchen to minister to the poor, more than thirty families left the church. Yet, through it all, when you see the expression on the face of one child who is able to eat, or one mom whose life is saved, one man to whom we are able to give a glimmer of hope, it is worth all the effort.

Helping hurting people is not without risk, danger, or frustration.

God never said that pulling people out of the ditch would be easy. The Samaritan had to physically lift the beaten, almost lifeless man onto his animal, all by himself. Have you ever tried to lift someone out of a ditch, or a hospital bed, or a hurt person off the floor? When a person is in a crumpled heap, they seem to weigh twice as much!

After struggling to get the beaten man onto the animal, the Samaritan took him to the inn. It cost him in time, money, and effort to care for the beaten man, and he had no guarantee that the man would survive or that anything good would ever come of it. In the story Jesus told, no mention is made of the beaten man even thanking the Samaritan. The Samaritan

Selfishness and greed often rear their ugly heads in opposition to compassion.

didn't do right expecting a thank you note or some other response; he simply did what God wanted him to do, and God blessed his efforts. But we should never be deceived into thinking that expressing compassion is without cost. Compassion always costs something, but it's worth it.

The priest and the Levite succumbed to the temptation of comfort and ease.

How to Keep Your Heart Sensitive

To avoid becoming insensitive to human needs, I often try to do "acts of kindness" when the television cameras aren't rolling, when it's just me and whomever God wants me to help. Jesus Himself did not help everybody during His life on Earth; in fact, Jesus said that the poor would always be with us, so I have learned to rely on God's direction regarding whom I should try to help. The most important aspect of helping other people is hearing the voice of God and following His instructions.

The most important aspect of helping other people is hearing the voice of God and following His instructions.

I was in Tulsa, Oklahoma, for a speaking engagement, and I sensed that God wanted me to help a homeless person while I had some extra time. Tulsa is a generous, thriving community, so, not surprisingly, many homeless people gravitate there, as well. Yet as I drove through some of the poorest sections of town, I sensed no specific direction from God.

I had almost resigned myself to the fact that I had misunderstood God's instructions, something that I've done on many occasions. When that happens, I simply go back to the Lord, and honestly admit, "Lord, I thought I understood what You wanted me to do in this situation, but apparently I missed something. Please re–direct my steps." The Lord has promised that if we will trust in Him and not lean on our own understanding, He will direct our paths, He'll make our crooked ways straight (Proverbs 3:5–6).

I pointed my car back toward the church where I was to speak, and along the way, I stopped at a gas station. In the restroom, a guy recognized me. "Hey! Aren't you on TV?"

I said, "Yes, I'm on TV. I'm Larry Jones, with Feed The Children. Maybe you've seen some of our programs."

"Yes, I have," he replied. My heart started pounding and I finally sensed the Spirit of God nudging me to help this man.

Right there in the gas station restroom, the man poured out his heart to me. He told me that he was a Christian who had fallen on hard times. He had traveled there to start a new job, but his new employment didn't begin until the next day. He needed twenty–two dollars to pay for his motel room that night. Little did he know that because God had already prepared my heart to help him, I would have paid almost any amount for his room, but he asked for twenty–two dollars, so that's what I gave him, plus eight dollars to get something to eat.

"I'll pay you back,' he said. "I'll send it to you. I promise you, sir."

"Listen, you just take this money, and when you have enough to pay me back, you give it to the next person who is in need."

The man went away praising God, and so did I! I did not help every homeless person in Tulsa that day. I helped one man who needed twenty–two dollars for his motel room that night. That was it, but it was God nudging me, so my job was to obey.

I drove away shaking my head, with tears in my eyes. "Lord, I just want to thank you," I prayed with a smile. "Of all places to meet someone in need—in a bathroom!"

Do What You Can

A woman came to see me one day because she wanted to do something to help Feed The Children.

"I was going to get married, but my fiancé left me— literally standing at the altar. Every time I open my drawer, I see this ring. Here's my fiancé's wedding ring," she said. "Please sell it and use the money to help feed some hungry children."

A few days later, I told that story on television and within a week, I received eleven more wedding rings through the mail.

The jilted bride took something negative in her life and allowed God to use it to help others. Her kind gesture spawned even more generosity from many other people. When you do what God directs you to do, it sets something in motion, and other people want to join you in the ditch, helping to pull people out.

Once someone donated some flooded land to Feed The Children. That's okay. We prayed about it, God made a way for us to sell it to some duck hunters, and we used the money to feed children.

Not all of us can give a discarded wedding ring or a piece of land, but we all have the ability to reach out to the twelve million children in America who struggle with hunger every day. And that's something we must do, indeed, are asked to do. When the United States Congress recently passed welfare reform legislation, they, in effect told the American public, "Government is no longer in the business of feeding people. The problem is now yours."

This means that it is up to people like you and me, along with charities and relief organizations, churches and synagogues, to secure a better future for our children. Every right implies a responsibility, every opportunity an obligation, and every possession a privilege. "I must do something" will always solve more problems then "Something must be done."

So open your eyes and begin to see the interruptions in your life as God's opportunities to work in and through you. Reach out and create your own unique way to take what life has dished out to you, and turn it into something that God can use to help others. He loves turning around circumstances and situations. As Joseph said to his brothers who had sold him into slavery as a teenager, but who years later bowed before him in Egypt: "You meant evil against me; but God meant it for good, in order to . . . save many people alive" (Genesis 50:20). God will use the interruptions in your life for your good and for the good of many others.

God's work done in God's way will never lack God's supply.
R. A. TORREY

A Good Investment

One of the joys of my life has been seeing the following Scripture proven over and over again: "He who has pity on the poor lends to the Lord, and He will pay back what he has given" (Proverbs 19:17). "How can I make a loan to God?" I wondered when I first read this verse. "God owns it all anyhow. Why would He ask me to loan to Him?"

As I studied the passage, I discovered that as we give to the poor, God regards that as a loan to Him, and the original language of the Scripture implies that He will pay back with interest—not simply so we can have more, but so we can give more! God loves poor people; He has poor people so we will help them. So why does God have us?

Giving of our money is not the only way to be compassionate, but for most of us it is a very tangible means of expressing our concerns. Your check stubs will reveal whether your compassion is active or inactive because where we spend our money is a good indicator of what we deem to be important. Perhaps that's why the great preacher Charles Spurgeon said, "Feel for others—in your pocket." It's not enough simply to empathize or feel sorry for those who are hurting. We must do something to help.

In our work at Feed The Children, and often in my own life, I am faced with enormous challenges and needs. I'm tempted to worry, and at those moments I must remind myself, "Whoa, Larry! This is not my work; it is God's. And He can take care of His "problems." My responsibility is to trust and to obey. I breathe a lot easier knowing that the battle is the Lord's. God always makes a way.

Our Story—His Story

When you really think about it, the story of the Good Samaritan is really our story, too. We've all been in our own ditches, but God graciously rescued us, and gave us a new start. Now it's our job to go back to the ditch, not as travelers beaten up along life's paths, but as Good Samaritans, reaching out to others with the love of Jesus Christ.

The ditch is full. Today another 35,000 children worldwide will die from starvation and diseases related to malnourishment [i]. Another twelve million American children will know the pangs of hunger again tomorrow. The Good Samaritan helped just one person, but he did help. We, too, must help the hurting around us, one person at a time.

In January 1979, Frances and I crawled into that full ditch with a nine–year–old boy, and we've never gotten out. The job is bigger than we are. Come and join us in the ditch. Allow God to interrupt your life. Our interruptions are always His opportunities!

He who gives his heart will not deny his money.
THOMAS FULLER, M.D.

The unfortunate need people who will be kind to them; the prosperous need people to be kind to.
ARISTOTLE

*A man is called selfish
not for pursuing his own good,
but for neglecting his neighbor's.*

RICHARD WHATELY

What Can I Do?

My child, I've often heard your question. This message is My answer.
You're concerned about the hungry in the world,
millions who are starving and you ask.
"What can I do?" FEED ONE.

You grieve for all the unborn children murdered every day and you ask,
"What can I do?" SAVE ONE.

You're haunted by the homeless poor who wander city streets and you ask,
"What can I do?" SHELTER ONE.

You feel compassion for those who suffer pain,
sorrow and despair and you ask,
"What can I do?" COMFORT ONE.

Your heart goes out to the lonely, the abused,
and the imprisoned and you ask,
"What can I do?" LOVE ONE.

Remember this, my child: two thousand years ago the world
was filled with those in need just as it is today, and when the helpless
and the hopeless called out to Me for mercy, I sent a Savior—
HOPE BEGAN WITH ONLY ONE.

He who sees a need and waits to be asked for help is as unkind as if he had refused it.

DANTE ALIGHIERI

[i] Pages 10, 35, 110, 121 based on figures from Feed The Children's fiscal year 2001, which ended Sept. 30, 2001.

[ii] Stan Mooneyham, Is There Life Before Death (Glendale, CA: Regal Books, a division of GL Publications, Ventura, CA, 1985), p. 12.

[iii] William Barclay, The Gospel of Luke, The Daily Study Bible Series, (Philadephia, PA: The Westminster Press, 1956 edition), p. 143.

[iv] Source: J. Paul Covert, Phoenix, AZ "Love Ministry"

You can contact Feed The Children at:

Feed The Children
Post Office Box 36
Oklahoma, OK 73101-0036
1-800-627-4556
www.FeedTheChildren.org

Discover how you can be a modern-day Good Samaritan.

I hope you and your family, congregation, business, and civic group are sensitive to human needs all around you. You can help.

All royalties from this book go to support the work of Feed The Children.

Feed The Children is a nonprofit, Christian, charitable organization providing physical, spiritual, educational, vocational/technical, psychological, economic, and medical assistance and other necessary aid to children, families, and persons in need in the United States and internationally.

Teach me to feel another's woe,
To hide the fault I see;
That mercy I to others show,
That mercy show to me.

ALEXANDER POPE